N

D1144208

Health and Social Care

GCSE

Liam Clarke

Edexcel

Success through qualifications

Published in 2002 by:
Nelson Thornes Ltd
Delta Place
27 Bath Road
CHELTENHAM
GL53 7TH
United Kingdom

02 03 04 05 06 / 10 9 8 7 6 5 4 3

A catalogue record for this book is available from the British Library

ISBN 0 7487 7072-0

Illustrations by Oxford Designers and Illustrators;
Cartoons by Woody Fox

Page make-up by Florence Production, Stoodleigh, Devon

Printed and bound in Scotland by Scotprint

Introduction

Welcome to the Edexcel GCSE in Health and Social Care (Double Award)! This book presents all the information that you will need to do well on this course and I hope you will find it interesting. The book has been designed to ensure you have all the knowledge you need to complete the Edexcel GCSE in Health and Social Care successfully. Before we start, you may have a few questions . . .

What is a GCSE in a vocational subject?

A GCSE in a vocational subject is a work-related qualification designed to provide you with a choice of routes into further education or employment.

A GCSE in Health and Social Care will:

- introduce you to the area of health and social care
- give you the technical knowledge, skills and understanding relating to health and social care
- show you some of the skills you will need for employment or further education or training
- help you take charge of your own learning and development
- provide different forms of learning and assessment to help motivate you to achieve your best!

What will I study?

GCSE in Health and Social Care has three units and you will look at things like:

- Who needs care and how do they get the right help?
- What is 'health and well-being' and how do you measure it?
- What sorts of things affect people's personal development and relationships?

This textbook is intended for students who need to have an understanding of the basic principles of the health, social care and early years services. For many of you this will be your first introduction to the health and social care area. However, I am sure that a number of you may have already worked voluntarily, looking after younger brothers and sisters or other members of the family, or helping older people or people with disabilities by shopping or doing some other important tasks to make life easier for them.

How will I be assessed?

For units one and two you will need to put together a portfolio of your work in a folder which will be marked by your teacher. Your portfolio will be filled with completed assignments and projects that your teacher has asked you to carry out.

For unit three you will be asked to complete a test.

What can I do when I've completed the Edexcel GCSE in Health and Social Care?

With a GCSE in Health and Social Care, depending on your grades, you will be able to progress to:

- an Advanced Level course, perhaps a GCE or VCE, GNVQ, BTEC First or National employment combined with further study such as an NVQ in Care or and NVQ in Early Years Care and Education.

There are many jobs in the health and social care area, such as nursing, child care, physiotherapy, medicine and home caring. This course will help you make informed decisions about what career you might like in the health and social care services, and also help your own personal development.

How is this book organised and how will the different features help me?

The book is broken down into the three units you must study. Each unit contains all the information you will need.

Each unit has a Unit Introduction and a mini-contents list for that unit. This will give you a quick guide to what is in the unit and will help you get easily to the information you need within that unit.

The Jargon Dragon will appear every now and again to explain key words and terminology that you might be unfamiliar with. It is important that you understand these words and terms.

The Find it Out feature suggests ways that you can do your own research and investigation.

Think it Through will help develop your research and investigation skills further. These skills will help you reach the higher grades.

Case Studies in each unit describe real life situations that people might find themselves in. By working through the questions at the end of each case study you will be able to apply the theory you have learned to real health, social care or early years situations.

A Glossary at the end of the book contains all the key words and terms defined in the Jargon Dragons throughout the book.

I hope you will find this book useful for your course. Good luck!

Acknowledgements

The author and publishers gratefully acknowledge help from the following people who provided thorough reviews of this textbook at manuscript stage:

Marilyn Billingham, Educational Advisor
Carol Hicks, Greenhill Comprehensive School, Pembrokeshire
Nerys Jones, The Alun School, Flintshire
Adrian Lamb, Irlam and Cadishead Community High School, Manchester.

We would also like to thank the following people and organisations for permission to reproduce photographs and other material:

Central Office of Information: p.99; The Dairy Council: p.106; The Department of Health: p.36; Department of the Environment, Transport and the Regions: p.101; Health Promotion England: p.93, 94, 101; National Drugs Helpline: p.102; Nuffield Nursing Homes Trust: p.31; The Welsh Drug and Alcohol Unit, the Welsh Office: p.103; Women's Royal Voluntary Service: p.29.

Every attempt has been made to contact copyright holders, and we apologise if any have been overlooked. Should copyright have unwittingly been infringed in this book, the owners should contact the publishers who will make corrections at reprint.

Photo credits
Photofusion: B. Apicella, p.77; Jean Attree, pp.2–3 Liam Bailey, p.7; Paul Baldesare, pp.8, 15 (top and bottom), 17, 46, 51, 83, 91; Bipichendra, p.112; Robert Brook, p.120; Mark Campbell, p.79; Paul Chitty, p.48; Paul Doyle, pp.10, 38 (top), 78, 146; Gina Glover, pp.81 (bottom), 84, 139, 171; Don Gray; p.173 Crispin Hughes, pp.4, 35, 38 (bottom), 41, 45, 177, 179; Tim Jones, p.141; Ute Klaphake, p.138 (bottom); Clarissa Leahy, pp.81 (top), 134; Caroline Mardoff, p.118; Julia Martin, pp.18 (top), 42, 67, 114 (bottom), 145, 158; Brian Mitchell, pp.18 (bottom), 20 (l and r); David Montford, pp.19, 144, 149, 155; G. Montgomery, pp.32, 100, 128; Peter Olive, pp.85, 114 (top), 143; Jon Spaull, p.175; Christa Stadtler, pp.50, 82, 153, 166, 169; Sam Tanner, p.178 David Tothill, pp.70–1, 87, 92, 96, 97; Bob Watkins, pp.33, 89, 130–1, 138 (top), 152, 162 (bottom); Libby Welch, p.44; Vicky White, p. 73

John Birdsall Photography: 9, 13, 14, 47, 164 (top), 168

John Walmsley Photography: pp.11, 161, 162 (top l and r) 164 (bottom),

Corbis UK Ltd, p.80

This unit will help you to:

understand more about how the health,
social care and early years services have
developed to meet government targets, as
well as the needs of individuals. It will also
help you understand the different services
that are provided and the jobs that people
carry out for individuals who use the
services.

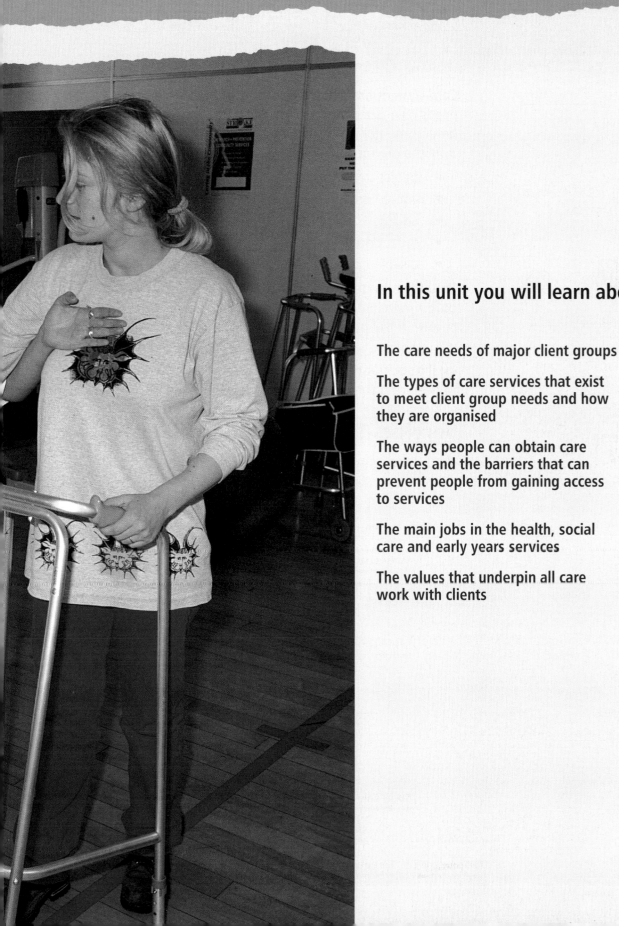

In this unit you will learn about:

The care needs of major client groups

Care services are designed to meet the health and social care needs of major client groups. Many of these groups also have developmental needs and you will find more about these in Unit 3. These client groups are:

- babies and children
- adolescents
- adults
- older people
- disabled people.

They are also designed to meet social policy goals set by the government, such as reducing poverty, homelessness and drug misuse in the population as a whole.

Health and local authorities have to assess the care needs of local populations in order to identify the services they are likely to need and the reasons why they seek them.

Services for babies and children

The following services are available for babies and children.

Services for children

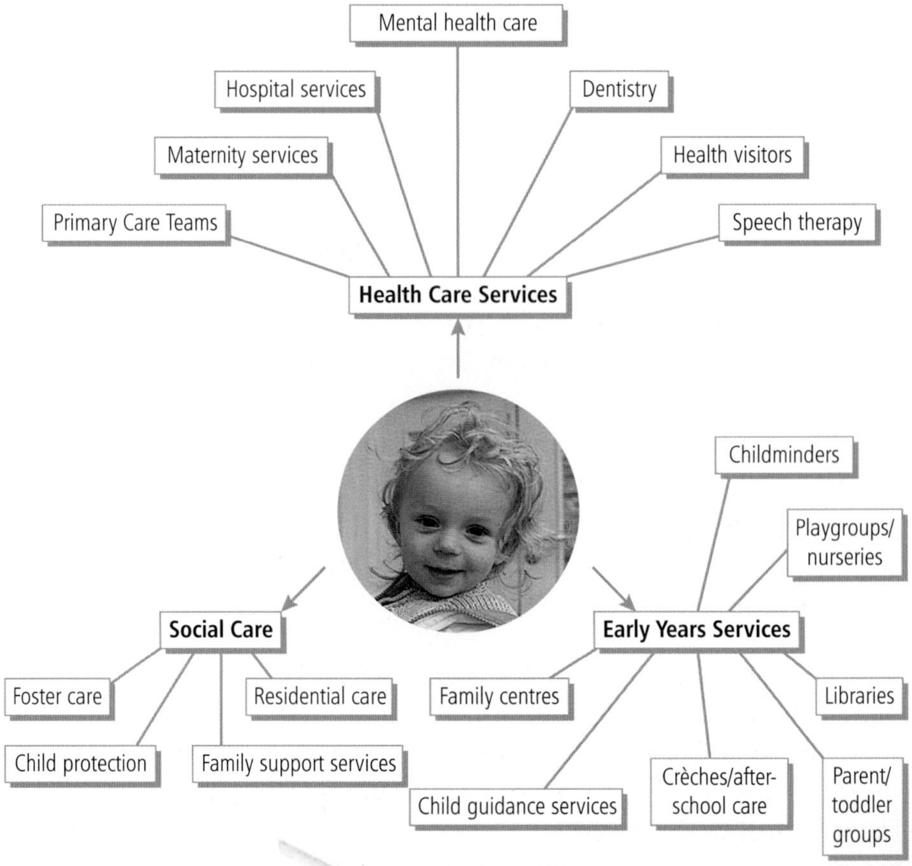

Mental health care

Hospital services

Dentistry

Maternity services

Health visitors

Primary Care Teams

Speech therapy

Health Care Services

Childminders

Playgroups/ nurseries

Social Care

Early Years Services

Foster care

Residential care

Family centres

Libraries

Child protection

Family support services

Crèches/after- school care

Parent/ toddler groups

Child guidance services

Health services for babies and children

The **Primary Care Team** provides the first level of health care and support for babies, children and their families. The team is made up of:

- health visitors
- general practitioners (GPs)/doctors
- practice nurses
- community/district nurses/midwives
- opticians
- pharmacists and
- dentistry services.

Primary Care Team – the first level health care team, made up of doctors, nurses and other support workers

The health care team

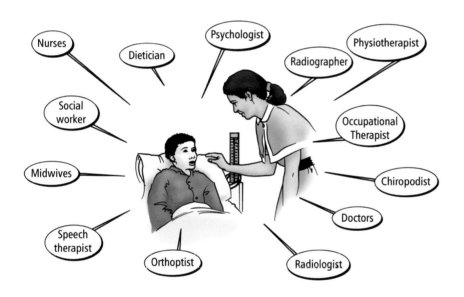

Other health and care workers are also available to this client group if they are in need of other kinds of support, such as physiotherapy or speech therapy. The jobs of all these care workers are described in detail later in this chapter.

For example, health visitors visit families with babies, to keep a check on the babies' development and offer care advice to parents. Health visitors are employed by the local health authority.

Education and early years services for babies and children

Education is vital to health and social care. It provides people with information, helps them to acquire skills and knowledge, and influences their values.

Education also plays an important part in developing people's identity, self-esteem and social skills. Formal education includes pre-school education, such as nurseries and playgroups, which provide important learning opportunities for young children.

Education or early years services for children should be based upon the following principles:

- parents should be involved in discussions and decisions about their children
- the needs and welfare of the children are most important
- all children have a right to play in a safe and stimulating environment
- services should take account of the needs of all children, whatever their gender, race, culture, language or disability.

Think
IT THROUGH

How can professional workers make sure they involve all the relevant people in the decision-making process? Why is it important that they do so? Which professional workers make decisions about education services for children?

The following early years and education services are available for children:

Day nurseries (private, voluntary and local authority) – Day nurseries look after children under the age of 5 for the length of the working day. A number are run by Social Services Departments or Education Departments, but voluntary groups, private companies or individuals also provide day nurseries.

Nursery schools/classes – Nursery schools may be independently run and are also attached to infant schools.

Playgroups – Playgroups provide sessions of care for children aged between 3 and 5. Some groups may take children at the age of $2^{1}/_{2}$. Playgroups aim to provide learning experiences through structured (this means *carefully managed*) play in groups. Many of these groups are run by one or two paid staff with the help of parents. A few playgroups are run by local authorities and some cater for children with special needs. Many playgroup sessions last for a morning or afternoon.

Activities in playgroups help children to learn

Childminders – Childminders look after children aged 3 months and over, during the working day. Parents and childminders decide between themselves how much the parents should pay. Childminders must be registered with the local Social Services Department.

Out of school clubs – Out of school clubs are available for children before and after school. Holiday schemes provide care all day during school holidays.

Family centres – Family centres provide a range of facilities for children, such as play sessions, toy libraries and out of school activities. They also help and advise adults with family problems. These centres can be attended by children of any age and their families. Many of these centres are run by the Family Welfare Society or Dr Barnado's, both of which are voluntary organisations.

What is a voluntary organisation? Look in your local Yellow Pages and make a list of some voluntary organisations in your area.

FIND
IT
OUT

Foster parents are recruited and trained by the Social Services Department

Social care services for babies and children

The following social care services are available for babies and children.

Foster care – Social Services Departments (and also a number of voluntary organisations) place babies and children in need with families or individuals who are able to offer full-time care in their own home. This care may be for a few days or much longer, according to the needs of the child.

Foster parents are recruited, approved and trained by the local Social Services Department. Foster parents work in partnership with social workers in looking after the needs of the child who is fostered. The local authority pays foster carers an allowance for looking after children.

Professional child care workers believe that, for most children, being with foster carers in a small family unit is better than being in a children's home (see below).

Residential care – Most residential care provision for children is now in the form of children's homes caring for small numbers of children. It has long been understood that large, long-stay institutions can harm children. Most children's residential care is

? *Analyse the advantages and disadvantages of placing a child in residential care compared to placement in a foster home.*

Think
IT THROUGH

now limited to custody of children referred (this means *sent*) by the courts or for assessment of their needs before going to court.

Child protection service – Child protection workers, such as social workers, doctors, pediatricians, health visitors and the police, make up the child protection services. The children's charity, the National Society for the Prevention of Cruelty to Children (NSPCC), may also be involved. Social workers play the lead role in child protection, but they work very closely with all the other agencies.

If the protection services think it is best for the children, they may be removed from the care of their parents and placed in residential care or foster care. A children's court will make the final decision after hearing all the evidence presented by social workers, police and doctors.

Social workers work with other agencies involved with child protection

case study

Khizar

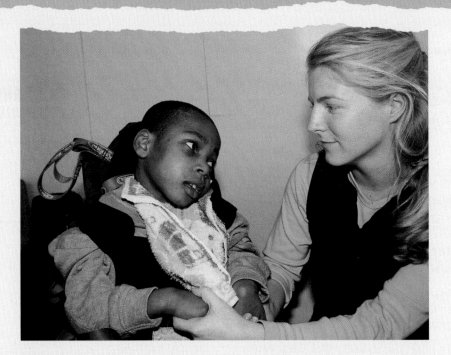

Khizar is 6. He has physical and learning difficulties. He was very bright and sociable until he had an road accident a year ago in which he suffered brain damage and also damaged his back. He now has to use a wheelchair.

When Khizar had the accident he was rushed to hospital in an ambulance after paramedics had given him treatment. He had an operation on his brain to remove a blood clot and his back was immobilised so that it could recover from the accident.

While in hospital Khizar was looked after by doctors who prescribed medicines, physiotherapists who helped him with movement and social workers who worked with him and his family. Khizar's social worker also helped him by talking about the accident to him and supporting him in making decisions about his life. An occupational therapist helped Khizar's family to decide what adaptations needed to be made to his home to allow him to live there after his discharge from hospital.

When he was discharged from hospital a community nurse visited to change his dressings and check up on his treatment. His GP was also informed of his discharge from hospital.

Khizar attends his local school where special arrangements have been made to accommodate his disability. Ramps have been built to allow him access to

case study

Khizar

the classrooms and a new toilet has been built for him. He also has the support of a classroom assistant.

Khizar is taken to school by a special bus and while in school he can call on a special care assistant who helps him go to the toilet.

Q *What has happened to Khizar? Explain in detail.*

Describe the changes that have been made in school to help Khizar.

Who has been involved in Khizar's treatment and care? Describe each professional's role and explain the informal care he would also receive.

Services for adolescents

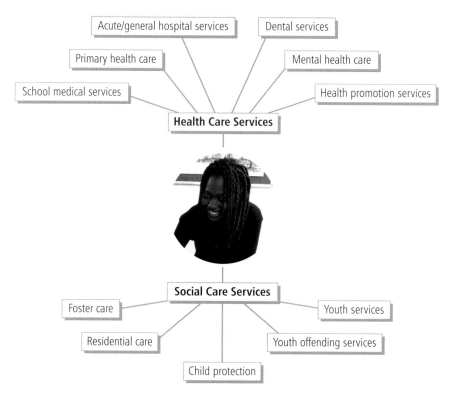

Services for adolescents

Acute/general hospital services
Dental services
Primary health care
Mental health care
School medical services
Health promotion services
Health Care Services

Social Care Services
Foster care
Youth services
Residential care
Youth offending services
Child protection

Many of the services used by children that were listed above are also available to support adolescents. Examples are foster care, residential care, child protection services and primary health services. However, some services are specific to the needs of adolescents and they are listed below.

School medical service – The school nurse is available to see children and adolescents. The nurse also provides a health education service to school students. The school nurse also provides information about the national immunisation (vaccination) programme.

Health promotion service – Health information offered to young people gives them the opportunity to make lifestyle choices that may affect their health. If young people are fully aware of the effects on health of smoking, drugs, unsafe sex or alcohol they may be less likely to use them.

FIND IT OUT

Find two leaflets, which advise adolescents about smoking, drug abuse or alcohol. Are the leaflets attractive and eye-catching? Did you learn anything new from them? Would you read them again? Were the messages clear?

Services for adults

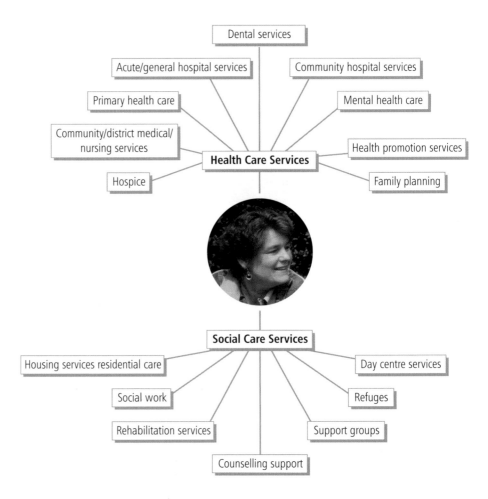

Health Care Services
- Dental services
- Acute/general hospital services
- Community hospital services
- Primary health care
- Mental health care
- Community/district medical/nursing services
- Health promotion services
- Hospice
- Family planning

Social Care Services
- Housing services residential care
- Day centre services
- Social work
- Refuges
- Rehabilitation services
- Support groups
- Counselling support

Services for adults

Many of the services used by children and adolescents, such as primary health services, health promotion, hospital services and residential care, are also available for adults. However, some services are specifically for adults and they are described below.

Housing for homeless families – Local authorities provide bed and breakfast accommodation, usually in hotels or hostels, for families who have been made homeless. A family may become homeless because, for example, the rent has not been paid, or because their home is uninhabitable through fire or flood.

Local authorities provide bed and breakfast accommodation for homeless families

Residential care – Residential care includes a number of services that are provided for people who have left their own homes for whatever reason. Residential care is often offered to people with physical disabilities, mental health difficulties, dependent persons (due to age or illness) and people with learning disabilities.

People receiving care in their own homes can usually have arrangements made to suit their own needs. The kind of care that each residential care facility offers depends on the needs of the residents who live there. Some elderly residents may take time to adjust to a new lifestyle: they may have to take their meals at certain times that they find inconvenient, or go to bed earlier than they might like to because there are not enough members of staff to take care of everyone's wishes. Residents may not have any choice over what to eat or which doctor they see.

On the positive side they will have security, companionship, and have their basic needs of food, shelter and warmth met.

THE JARGON DRAGON

empowerment – enabling people to make decisions for themselves

Domiciliary care – Domiciliary care is care offered to people living in their own home. People receive these services, whether home carer or meals-on-wheels, when rehabilitating from illness or in the long term because of their dependency needs. People who are frail and dependent may wish to stay in their own home rather than enter residential care.

People benefit from living in their own home, as they may be near friends and relatives, and can go to bed or eat meals when they like. They are allowed to make decisions for themselves; this is known as **empowerment**.

However, there may be some disadvantages of living at home when dependent on others. Care staff may not be available to get people up out of bed in the morning or help put them to bed at times they wish. Friends may not be living near, and relatives and family may live far away or have died.

Counselling services – Counselling helps people to understand and come to terms with, and then cope with their problems. The main aim is to help people to use their own experience and understanding of how they feel about their situation, and so enable them to take control of their own life. Counsellors give guidance and support on an individual basis or in a group situation.

Counselling works best when specific needs have been identified, for example, bereavement, family relationship issues or divorce. Counsellors also give advice on careers and finance.

Counsellors can help couples with relationship issues

Services for older people

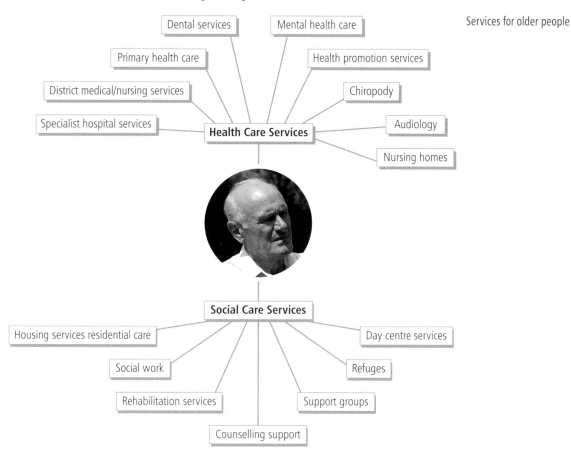

Services for older people

Dental services

Mental health care

Primary health care

Health promotion services

District medical/nursing services

Chiropody

Specialist hospital services

Health Care Services

Audiology

Nursing homes

Social Care Services

Housing services residential care

Day centre services

Social work

Refuges

Rehabilitation services

Support groups

Counselling support

Many services used by children, adolescents and adults are available to support the older person, such as primary health services, health promotion, hospital services and residential care. However, some services are specific to the needs of older people, as explained below.

A day centre provides a place for social recreation for older people, and may provide stimulating activities such as this local history class

It must be remembered that, although older people may have poorer health than younger people, ageing itself does not cause disease. Older people with good health habits and who undertake regular physical activity stay healthier for longer. For most older people the benefits of activity outweigh the risk. The majority of older people require either no care or care only occasionally.

Improving standards of living and medical advances mean that many more people are living longer. A man born in Britain in 1901 could expect to live for an average of 45 years and a woman for nearly 50 years. A woman born today can expect to live for 80 years and a man for 75 years. This means that the people who manage health and social care services have to decide how to meet the needs of all these people who are living longer lives.

More and more people need more support, and current levels of health and social services care for older people in their own homes are not sufficient to be a reliable alternative to residential care. All the research on provision of support services to older people highlights the importance of the family. The decline of the family unit, with families split up or living far apart, means that fewer older people will be able to be looked after by relatives. This will put increased pressure on day care and domiciliary services.

Maria is an older lady who is very confused. She has lived alone in a large house for many years since her husband died. She managed to cope on her own until she suffered a fall and damaged her hip. Since her fall she has become more and more confused, and sometimes does not recognise the postman or milkman. She also sometimes leaves the gas on without lighting it. An occupational therapist has recommended aids and adaptations to her home and a physiotherapist comes in to help her move her affected leg.

She has no relatives. She has difficulty getting her pension every week. She is now so frail that she can no longer cook her own meals and because of her hip injury cannot get in or out of bed without the help of a home carer.

The care team that would help and support Maria

Q *Explain what has happened to Maria.*

Describe the role of each professional in the team caring for Maria.

What do you think will happen to Maria now?

Services for people with disabilities

Services for people with disabilities

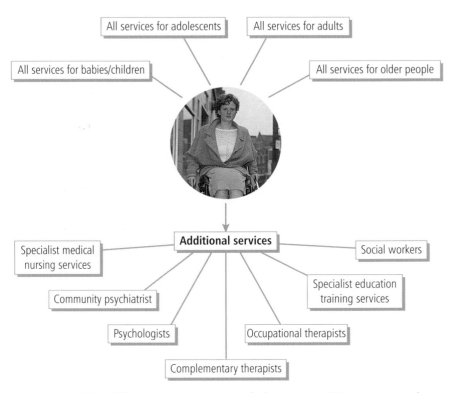

All services for adolescents

All services for adults

All services for babies/children

All services for older people

Additional services

Specialist medical nursing services

Social workers

Community psychiatrist

Specialist education training services

Psychologists

Occupational therapists

Complementary therapists

Around 1.3 million people, most of them over 65, are severely or permanently disabled. Over 200,000 people in England alone are blind or partially sighted. Many of these people are cared for in residential homes.

All individuals need love, security, safety, nutrition, warmth and intellectual fulfilment. However, people with physical and mental disabilities may have additional needs relating to their condition. For example they may have mobility needs, or they may need help with speech, vision or hearing.

A wheelchair enables a person with disabilities to be mobile

The basic needs of all age groups are similar, but needs do change over a person's lifetime. Advancing age, illness, physical or mental disabilities, and social, emotional and financial problems all affect an individual's needs.

What basic social and emotional needs would be met by a care worker supporting a disabled person living in their own home?

Think
IT THROUGH

The main legislation (this means *laws*) that enables local authorities to support people with disabilities in the community is the Chronically Sick and Disabled Persons Act 1970. For the purposes of the Act, chronically sick or disabled persons are those who are 'substantially and permanently handicapped' by illness, injury, congenital deformity (disability a person is born with) or old age. The Act enables the local authority to provide:

- practical assistance in the home, such as help with obtaining radio, telephone, TV or library services
- works or adaptations in the home
- assistance with holidays
- provision of meals at home.

Defining disability

There are many types of disability and the term cannot be defined easily. Disabilities may be the result of the following factors. Find out about the conditions mentioned if you do not know what they are:

- genetic or inherited disorders, such as Down's syndrome
- damage at birth, such as cerebral palsy
- accidents (causing brain damage or paralysis, for example)
- illnesses (such as bronchitis) or disorders (such as Alzheimer's disease) that have developed during a person's lifetime.

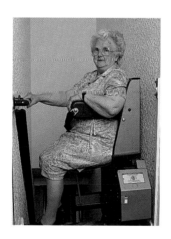

A stairlift enables an older person to be mobile and live in their own home

In a group discuss and agree on a definition of disability.

Think
IT THROUGH

THE JARGON DRAGON

chronic disability – a condition that develops slowly over a long period, lasts a long time or may be incurable

acute disability – condition that occurs suddenly, may be severe and may last for a relatively short time

congenital disability – a non-hereditary condition that a person is born with

FIND IT OUT

Disability may be either:

- physical – arthritis, chronic heart disease, blindness, deafness; or
- mental – learning difficulties in children, such as Down syndrome or cerebral palsy, or Alzheimer's disease or dementia in older people.

Each person will be affected differently by their disability. When thinking about support services for people with disabilities it is important to remember that each client is an individual and to focus on their individual needs, both physical and emotional, rather than on their disability.

For example, some people with disabilities may be able to cope and live at home, while others with the same disability may need much more support and may even need residential care.

> *Mandy is 30. She is losing her sight. What organisations could help and support her?*

Any of the services described in this unit can meet the needs of people with disabilities, but in addition to the services that are used by everyone, people with disabilities may need specialist services, such as specialist medical or nursing care, occupational therapists, or specialist education and training services.

People with disabilities benefit from support from physiotherapists

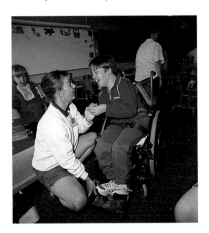

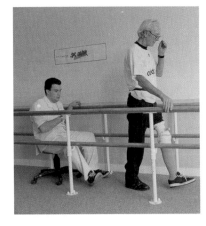

Older people with disabilities

Many 'old' old people (over 85) live alone and see no relatives or friends for long periods. They are more likely to need domiciliary care from home helps and other support, such as meals-on-wheels and the services of a **chiropodist**. They also need regular support from their health visitor and social workers. Many are also likely to need to stay in hospital for periods of time.

THE JARGON DRAGON

chiropodist – a trained professional who looks after people's feet

Even the simplest illness may be serious for an older person. This may be because of other conditions they are suffering at the same time, such as:

- decline of their mental powers
- loneliness
- accidents and falls
- rheumatism/arthritis
- foot defects – 50 per cent of older people have some foot problems, such as ingrown toenails, corns and bunions
- hypothermia (where the body's temperature falls too low)
- cardiovascular (heart) disease
- hearing loss
- visual defects
- nutrition problems
- bronchitis
- prostate problems (in men).

Find out what these conditions are if you do not know.

The types of care services that exist to meet client group needs and how they are organised

The 1990s saw one of the biggest changes in the organisation of the health and social care services since the National Health Service was set up in 1948. Care services can be split up in the following way:

- statutory care services – the National Health Service and Social Services of the local authority
- voluntary care sector services
- private care sector services.

On the charts below, you will find set out both the statutory and non-statutory health and social care services you may come across. Remember, statutory services are set up under legislation (laws). Some services may be provided by either statutory or non-statutory bodies.

Statutory services

National Health Service	Social Services of the local authority
General practitioners (GPs)	Residential care services
Hospital services	Domiciliary care
Community nursing services	Day care services
Nursing homes	Meals-on-wheels
Ambulance services	Aids and adaptations
	Child protection services

Local authority	Private/voluntary/independent
Luncheon clubs	Residential care
Respite care (holidays)	Nursing care
Meals services	Meals-on-wheels
Aids to daily living	Residential care
	Day care
	Playgroups
	Day nurseries
	Social workers (NSPCC)

Statutory services

The National Health Service and Social Services of the local authority form the statutory sector of the health and social care services. They are described as 'statutory' because they were set up by Acts of Parliament and are funded by public money.

National Health Service

The structure of the health services is based around the National Health Service (NHS), which was formed in 1948 by the National Health Service Act. This Act brought the health services (hospitals, hospital doctors, GPs, nurses), and in particular the hospitals, under the control of the Ministry of Health.

The government department responsible for delivering health care is the Department of Health. The department monitors standards through eight regional offices and takes steps to deal with services that are failing to meet demands.

The Regional Health Authorities monitor Health Authorities. Health Authorities identify the health needs of local people, and make arrangements for services to be provided by NHS Trusts, Primary Care Trusts and other organisations, using funds provided by the government. All the bodies that make up NHS England 2002 are described below.

NHS England 2002

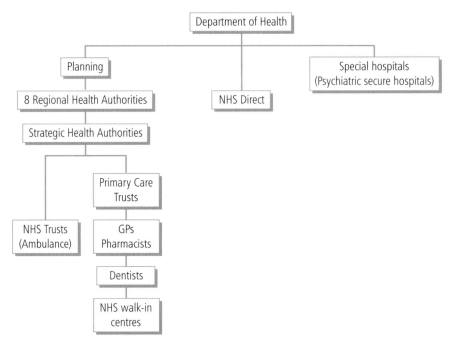

Primary care – The first port of call for many people when they develop a health problem is their local GP. Each UK citizen has a right to be registered with a local GP and visits to the local surgery are free. GPs are at the front line of the NHS, the part officially called 'primary care'. Many other professionals are part of the Primary Care Team, including nurses, health visitors, dentists, opticians and pharmacists. NHS Direct and walk-in centres also form part of primary care.

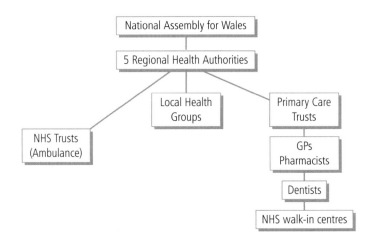

Visit your local library or use the internet, www.open.gov.uk, to find out what health care trusts are operating in your locality.

NHS Wales 2002

Local Health Groups (LGHs) have been set up in Wales by the Welsh Assembly. They have been established in each area to provide a focus for the development and improvement of services. LGHs are committees of the Health Authorities.

In Northern Ireland, there are Health and Social Services Boards that provide both health and personal social services under one manager. Health and Social Services Boards:

- assess what people need
- negotiate contracts for their care services with other organisations
- make sure that services are accessible
- monitor services
- plan and develop new services
- demonstrate value for money on all services.

The Health Act 1999 – In 1997 the government set out to change the structure of the NHS in order to provide an up-to-date, quicker and more responsive service, based on people's needs, not their ability to pay. The government outlined its plans in a White Paper called *The New NHS Modern Dependable*. Briefly, the government's aims are as follows:

- To make it easier and faster for people to get advice and information about health, illness and the NHS, so that people can care for themselves and their families better. To help with this the government has set up <u>NHS Direct</u>, a 24-hour telephone and internet service staffed by nurses, which is now available in all areas of the UK.
- Quick advice and treatment in the community in local surgeries and health centres, with GPs working alongside other health care staff to provide a wide range of services.
- Prompt access to specialist services in hospital, linked to local surgeries and health centres.

Walk-in centres – NHS walk-in centres offers fast access to health advice and treatment. They are available to anyone and provide:

- a seven-days-a-week service
- assessment by an experienced nurse
- treatment for minor injuries and illnesses
- access to health advice and information
- information on local out-of-hours GP and dental services
- information on pharmacy services.

There are now over 40 walk-in centres in the UK.

THE JARGON DRAGON

NHS Direct – staffed by nurses and trained operators, a telephone service giving advice and immediate information on what to do and not to do in an emergency, at any time of day or night. Phone 0845-4647, www.nhsdirect.nhs.uk

FIND IT OUT

Contact the nearest walk-in centre to you. What services are provided there?

Think IT THROUGH

Why did the government introduce the reform of the health service in 1999? You will find useful information on the Department of Health's website, www.doh.gov.uk

Strategic Health Authorities – Strategic Health Authorities have replaced the old District Health Authorities. Each Strategic Health Authority will serve a population of approximately 1.5 million people.

Strategic Health Authorities work with local authorities, NHS Trusts and Primary Care Trusts to produce Health Improvement Programmes to provide the framework within which all NHS bodies operate.

The key roles of Strategic Health Authorities are to:

- find out the health needs of the local population and develop a strategy for meeting those needs
- decide what services are necessary to meet local needs
- allocate resources (money) to Primary Care Trusts and make sure that Primary Care Trusts work properly.

Primary Care Trusts – As part of the government's plan to make the service more responsive to local needs, a system of Primary Care Trusts has been set up. Primary Care Trusts, made up of GPs, community nurses and others, such as social workers and home carers, work with other NHS Trusts to deliver quick, accessible, co-ordinated care of a high standard. These groups work to set standards agreed with Strategic Health Authorities. Primary Care Trusts replaced the old Primary Care Groups and Hospital and Community NHS Trusts.

A board comprising GPs, nurses, managers, Social Services representatives and members of the public manages Primary Care Trusts. This is to ensure that there is co-operation and co-ordination between health and social services. It is hoped that the Social Services and the NHS will come together with new agreements to pool resources. <u>Primary Care Trusts</u> will eventually purchase nearly 90 per cent of hospital and community care.

Health Action Zones – To give priority to areas of greatest need the government has set up Health Action Zones to help reduce inequalities. Health Action Zones bring together local health organisations with local authorities, community groups, voluntary groups and local business to provide improved health for local people.

Patient Advocacy and Patients Forum – Each Primary Care Trust has a Patient Advocacy and Liaison Service (PALS) that patients and carers can turn to in order to resolve problems as and when they arise, rather than just helping patients to complain after the event has occurred. This service replaced the Community Health Councils which provided advice and support for patients and their families.

Each Primary Care Trust also has a Patients Forum made up of patients and representatives from patient and voluntary groups, with the power to visit Trust hospital premises to check on standards, including cleanliness and food.

THE JARGON DRAGON

Primary Care Trusts – bodies set up to plan and deliver local health care services

Statutory service – service set up by the government under legislation (law). Examples are the NHS and Social Services Departments

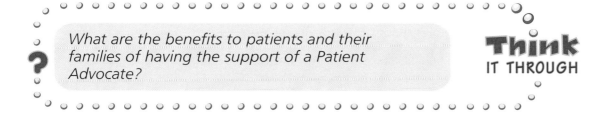

? *What are the benefits to patients and their families of having the support of a Patient Advocate?*

Think IT THROUGH

Social Services (*statutory service*)

Social Services Departments are responsible for the following health and social care needs:

- child care (this is controlled by the various Children Acts and Adoption Acts)
- provision and inspection of residential accommodation
- provision of welfare services for older people, people with disabilities and those who are chronically ill
- support of people suffering from mental illness (these powers are given by the Mental Health Acts).

The structure of a typical Social Services Department in England and Wales

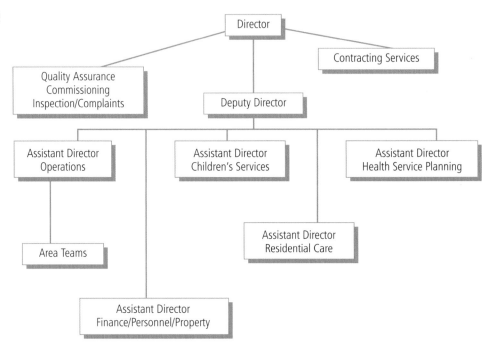

Social Services Departments also have powers to give other organisations (such as voluntary groups) responsibilities to provide services (such as residential care) on their behalf.

The organisation of local authority Social Services Departments has recently been changed by the National Health Service and Community Care Act. As with the health services (see above), the Act split up Social Services Departments into two parts:

- the part that buys the care needed and
- the part that provides that care.

The Act also stated that the care could be bought from the private and voluntary sectors.

The voluntary care sector

The term voluntary care sector refers to all non-statutory organisations that contribute to social care. Non-statutory means they are not set up by government. Many are charities, such as Age Concern, NSPCC and Barnardo's.

The setting up of charitable voluntary organisations in the nineteenth century was the start of social care and social work in an organised way. Early examples of such care include prison visiting and children's services. Many charities raise money to provide for people with specific needs. The money is then used to purchase the equipment or care required. Some charities, such as Anchor, provide specific residential accommodation for older people around the country.

WRVS is one of the UK's largest voluntary services, working to support families and older people in need

While some charities work with many unpaid volunteers, most are staffed almost totally by salaried workers. The term voluntary refers to the status of the organisation and not to the status of the workers.

Organisations in the voluntary sector range from the very large, like Age Concern, to very small local groups that deal with one specific need, such as transport to the local hospital. Voluntary organisations work alongside the statutory services providing care. A voluntary organisation can be paid by the NHS or a local authority to provide care.

> *Arrange to visit one local voluntary organisation and give a short presentation to the class on your findings.*

FIND IT OUT

Voluntary organisations provide many services, such as:

- mental health support
- support for people with disabilities
- meals-on-wheels
- home carers
- voluntary hospital transport
- housing
- child care services

- services for people with visual and physical impairments
- home visiting
- nursing services in the home and
- many more services at local level.

The private sector

Many organisations involved in health and social care charge for their services with the intention of making money. These commercial organisations are part of the private sector. Childcare provision is mostly private. There are also individuals working as private nurses, physiotherapists or care assistants to provide care in people's own homes.

Private organisations may bid (this means *put in a quote in competition with other organisations*) to provide care, such as residential care for older people (they then become a provider). The local authority can buy places in a home for people in need of the care.

Private health care

When the NHS was formed in 1948, many health professionals wanted to retain their freedom to charge for services outside the NHS. It was agreed that doctors would be allowed to work both within the NHS and in private practice. Private health care is available within:

- NHS-owned institutions, with the patient paying for the services
- totally separate private health care facilities.

The New Labour government in 2002 is encouraging partnerships between the private and public sector. Private money is being used to build NHS hospitals and NHS patients are being sent to private hospitals for treatment.

Nuffield Hospitals

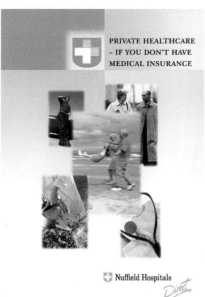

Nuffield Hospitals *Direct*

Private organisations provide a number of different care services

Ways of obtaining care services and barriers to access

How people gain access to services and use them

In order to use the different care services, people need to know about them and how to make contact with them. This section will explain how people are referred to different care services and the barriers that they may have to overcome to use the service.

There are four ways in which a person can be referred to the care services: <u>self-referral</u>, professional referral, compulsory referral and third-party referral. They are described below.

Self-referral

This is often the first route for people receiving health and social care. Within the health service, this may be by simply turning up at the doctor's or dentist's surgery. Within social care, referral may be to a local office, or direct to a care or early years facility, such as a daycare centre or a nursery.

THE JARGON DRAGON

self-referral – where people seek help themselves. This may involve support from family members

People are often first referred to care services by their doctor

THE JARGON DRAGON

professional referral – a doctor, social worker, nurse, teacher or other professional requests care or treatment for an individual from the social or medical services

compulsory referral – people who are unable to make a decision for themselves through mental illness or youth are placed into hospital or other care on the recommendation of a professional

In all cases, the person requiring care (or a friend or relative on their behalf) makes the first contact. For example, the mother of a child might enquire about a place in a day nursery.

Professional referral

Planned access to hospital care is usually by referral from a doctor. Where a doctor suspects ill-health that requires specialist treatment, the patient is referred to an out-patient clinic or, in more urgent cases, direct admission to a hospital may be arranged.

In the area of social care, an example of **professional referral** could be when a teacher in a school suspects child abuse and refers the case to the duty social worker in the Social Services Department. Another example could be when the police have given an official warning to a child who has committed an offence and they then refer the child to Social Services.

Compulsory referral

There are some cases where a person can be the subject of **compulsory referral** into hospital or other care. This is where a professional, such as a doctor or a social worker, identifies a person who is unable to make a decision for themselves, and effectively makes the decision for them. This may be because the person is too young or unable to make a decision because of mental ill-health.

Third party referral

This type of referral occurs when a person is put in touch with a social or health service by a friend or neighbour who is not employed as a professional carer.

Jack had been a teacher. Soon after he retired, his family noticed that his behaviour had altered. He was forgetting things that had just happened, but he was able to talk about his teaching as if it was still happening. His doctor noticed some increase in his confusion, but he always asked Jack basic questions requiring only yes or no answers.

Eventually Jack became so confused that his wife, Joan, was becoming very concerned. She spent a lot of time looking after him, and could not easily go to Social Services in the nearest town, which was 10 miles away, for help.

The situation changed when Joan developed a chest infection. The doctor wanted to refer Joan to hospital but was surprised when she asked, 'Who will look after Jack?' This was the first time the doctor had realised Jack was becoming seriously ill with Alzheimer's disease.

The doctor contacted the hospital to arrange for Joan to be admitted. At the same time, he contacted Social Services to arrange for Jack to move temporarily into residential care.

Q *What kind of referral was Joan's referral to her doctor?*

What type of referral was Joan's referral to hospital?

What kind of referral was Jack's referral to residential care?

Barriers to access to care

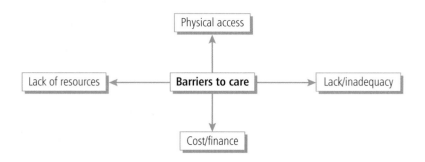

Lack of or inadequate information

The first barrier to receiving care is lack of knowledge. If you do not know what is available or how to ask for support, your chances of meeting your needs are low.

To ensure that people know what is available, the health and social services organisations provide publicity about what they do and their resources. This is available in a wide variety of places that are regularly visited by the public, including:

- health centres
- surgeries
- libraries
- colleges and schools
- Citizens' Advice Bureaux
- post offices
- council information offices
- Thomson directories, Yellow Pages and the phone book.

Most of this publicity will be in the form of printed leaflets or posters, usually with photographs and diagrams to make them look more interesting. Their aim is to tell you about the services available. Other information about health and social care frequently appears in newspapers. For example, annual reports of how different services are meeting charter standards (see below) are published and made available to the public.

There are two other important sources of information about services:

- the people who work in the service and
- people who have already used the service.

It is often the first source of information that is the most difficult to find, but once a client has gained access to care, the door is open to a network of information about caring services.

The first source can very often be someone who has already received care or the carers themselves. When a person first makes use of a health or care service, the people delivering the care are able to pass on information about other services available.

Charter standards – Since 1990 caring organisations have had to produce charters. These are documents that explain the standards of service that a client can expect, including how long clients have to wait for treatment. The individual services also publish figures to show how well they are meeting the standards set down in these charters. These statistics can be used by clients and care professionals to help them to choose the best services.

From April 2002 a new set of standards, referred to as National Minimum Standards, was used to monitor social care services and private health care.

> **?** *Mrs Patel is 87. She is Asian and English is not her first language. What difficulties do you think she might encounter in trying to access medical services?*

Think IT THROUGH

Adapting communication to meet client needs –
Most of the information that you have found about services available will have been written down, but most caring services adapt their communications to meet the needs of different groups of people. For example, most leaflets are available in the major languages spoken by people living in the area. Where people do not speak English well, many services also employ people to act as interpreters.

Interpreters can help with communication

'Your Guide to the NHS' sets out standards that patients can expect and explains what services are available

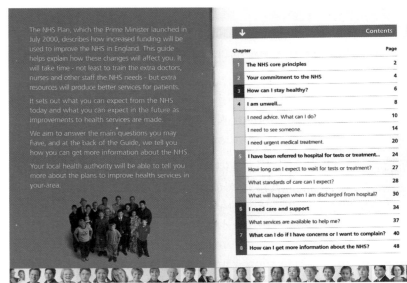

THE JARGON DRAGON

Braille – words written as a code of raised dots, read by some people with visual impairment

The two other languages that are important in providing care information are **Braille** for people with impaired or no sight and sign language for people who are deaf or have imp[aired hearing. Written information for visually impaired people who have some vision is also available in large print.

Location of information – Sometimes it might be necessary to place posters and leaflets in specific places in order to reach particular groups of people. For example, it would be more effective to place a poster advertising a new clinic for drug users in a place where drug users are likely to go.

FIND IT OUT

Visit your local library or doctor's surgery and look at the information leaflets there. How many different languages are they written in?

Lack of resources

Heavy demand – Demand for a service may be a barrier if there are not enough services to meet that demand. For example, the demand for beds in a hospital for older people will rise during cold weather and all except emergencies may have to be placed on the waiting list.

Waiting lists – Waiting lists are also a potential barrier to access. Patients may have to wait for very long periods of time before treatment and may even die before treatment is available.

Physical barriers

A major difficulty of gaining access to buildings can be the steps at the front door. Many people with disabilities have difficulties walking up steps. If all new buildings had to have ramps instead of steps then the access problem would be solved!

> *Is there good access for people in wheelchairs at your school, your local shopping centre and leisure centre?*

FIND IT OUT

Some thought and simple changes can remove barriers to physical access

Financial and cost barriers

Care today is not free. Even when a friend or unpaid volunteer is providing the care, they are paying – with their time.

In the UK much health care is not charged for at the point of delivery (this means *when it is received and when the service is used*). However, it is paid for by everyone through general taxation and National Insurance contributions.

There are some services for which the client still has to pay all or part of the costs. The payments may be affected by the client's age or ability to pay. If you are under 18, for example, you may not have had to pay for any services yet, and retired people do not have to pay for most basic services. Contributions from clients for NHS services are required for:

- prescriptions for medicines
- prescriptions for appliances, such as surgical corsets

Eyesight tests and glasses are not free for all clients

- dental checks and treatment
- eyesight tests, glasses and contact lenses
- transport to and from hospital (in many cases)
- the costs of transport and treatment following a road accident
- some medical checks and vaccinations for business purposes.

Parents may have to pay for early years services

Paying for social care – Local authority social care often requires some payment to be made. Generally payment levels are assessed on the basis of income. Here age is not a factor and so older people with savings are not exempt from the payments. Some care services that normally require some contribution from the client include:

- day nurseries
- residential care (although not for children)
- day care
- domiciliary care (home helps/home carers)
- meals-on-wheels.

Paying for residential care – There are very many residential and nursing homes in the private sector. Until recently, the fees for many residents who could not pay for their care were met by the Department of Social Security (DSS). However, the increasing numbers of people requiring residential care means that there will not be enough money to pay for all who need care. People are now being advised to take out insurance to pay for residential care. This is because it is unlikely that the statutory sector will be able to provide sufficient care for those who cannot pay in the future.

Paying for care in the private sector – Private sector care requires payment. This payment can be made:

- by the client
- by an insurance company
- by the statutory services (where the care has been bought by the GP for example).

Private health care is often paid for by insurance companies where the client pays regular contributions to the company to insure against treatment costs.

Cost of the service – When thinking about the cost of the service, the following issues need to be considered.

- If clients have to pay for care themselves, can they afford it?
- Do the local services have enough money to provide the care needed by everyone in their area?
- Does the government have enough money to provide for everybody's care?

Where a service has to be paid for by a client, costs will often be difficult to meet. For people who receive social security benefits, there may be no charges, but people with low wages may find the costs too great.

There are more older people in the UK than ever before. The number of people paying National Insurance and income tax is not going to be sufficient to pay for all the services that are needed. The people who manage the caring services have to make decisions about the amount of care available. They also have to decide on which care is most important. When such decisions have to be made there are bound to be some people who do not get the care they need.

The problem of funding care has been recognised by the NHS and Community Care Act. The Act states that people can expect to have their care needs assessed but that they have no right to have the needs met. For example, a person may have been assessed as needing a home help every day, but may be offered help on just two days a week because there are not enough home carers to go around.

The main jobs in the health, social care and early years services

Health care staff

Of the staff who work within the NHS, 68 per cent are direct care workers (those who actually provide the care) and 32 per cent are management and support staff.

Direct care workers	Indirect care workers
Social worker	Medical receptionist
Home care assistants (home helps)	Cleaner
Meals-on-wheels staff	Hospital porter
Hospital doctor	Hospital reception staff
Hospital nurse	Hospital manager
General practitioner	Security staff
Practice nurse	GP health centre manager
District /community nurse	Clerical staff
Health visitor	Cook
Midwife	Ambulance driver
School nurse	Voluntary car driver
Community psychiatric nurse	Maintenance staff
Radiographers	
Physiotherapist	
Occupational therapist	
Speech therapist	
Chiropodist	
Nursery nurse	
Classroom assistant	

Some of the individual jobs are discussed below.

Hospital doctors

Nearly 10 million referrals are made to hospitals in the UK for treatment each year.

In hospitals patients are looked after by teams of doctors, who specialise in particular areas, such as paediatrics (children), obstetrics (childbirth) and geriatrics (older people). The role of hospital doctors is to:

- diagnose – find out what is wrong with the patient
- prescribe – decide on the treatment to help the patient
- monitor – review the condition of the patient and change the treatment if necessary.

Patients are usually referred to hospital doctors by their GPs. If patients need an operation, this is carried out by a surgeon.

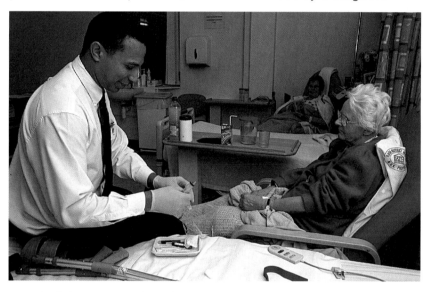

Hospital doctors regularly review the condition of patients in their care

Hospital doctors work with other professionals, such as nurses, physiotherapists and social workers. Together they are known as the multidisciplinary team. The senior doctors in the team may be referred to as specialists or consultants, or may be called 'medical director'.

Hospital nurses

Most nurses are to be found working in hospitals alongside doctors. There are two levels of personnel in the nursing team currently employed in the NHS:

- registered general nurses (RGNs): nurses specialise in areas such as renal (care of kidney patients), onocology (cancer patients), neurology (working with people with brain damage), cardiology (working with heart patients) or children's nursing. They will need additional training for this work
- health care assistants (HCAs), who support the RGNs.

General practitioners

GPs are just one part of the front line of the NHS and work in that part of the service called Primary Care. Most services offered by GPs are free to patients, although there are charges for prescriptions and such things as vaccinations for overseas travel.

A hospital nurse may decide to specialise in caring for children

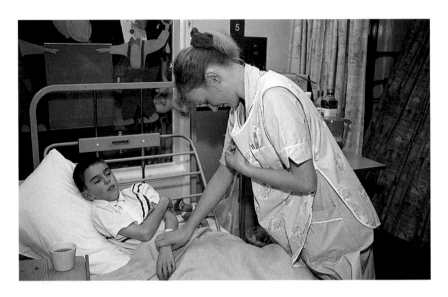

Children, older people and those on low income receive prescribed medicines for free.

Most people select their own general practitioner (GP) when they are over 16 years old.

It has now become very common for several GPs to work together in group practices. Within the group practice are GPs, receptionists, administrative staff and probably a practice nurse and a social worker employed by the practice. Health visitors may also be based in GP practices.

Practice nurses

The practice nurse is usually employed directly by a GP practice, where most of his or her work is carried out. The practice nurse carries out such tasks as changing dressings, doing urine tests and administering injections.

The practice nurse may run 'well woman' and 'well man' clinics, and may also offer a counselling service to patients and relatives.

FIND IT OUT

What are 'well woman' and 'well man' clinics?

District/community nurses

Primary Care Trusts have a responsibility to provide nurses to assist with treatment in a patient's home, providing support and nursing care for acute and chronic patients of all ages, mainly for older people in their own homes. District and community nurses are employed by local health authorities.

They also provide the link between hospitals and the Primary Care Team by referring patients to other carers and services.

Health visitors

The health visitor is an RGN with post-graduate training and the Health Visitor's Certificate. The role of the health visitor is in the area of:

- health education
- prevention of illness and promotion of health in antenatal classes and health clinics
- monitoring the development of children with parents in the family home.

The health visitor also has a large part to play in the community care of older people.

Visit your careers teacher and look at the information leaflets on jobs in the health services. Make notes on the qualifications for the different kinds of work that the various professionals do.

Midwives

Midwives are independent, professional nurses in their own right. They are responsible for supervising antenatal and postnatal care of all women, whether they are to have their baby in hospital or in their own home.

They also look after the mother and baby for 10 days after birth.

Midwives may be based in the community or in a hospital. There are approximately 5000 midwives working in the community in the UK.

School nurses

The school nurse promotes positive attitudes to health within the education system by:

- giving advice on health matters to school staff
- looking after the children
- carrying out screening checks (checking for headlice for example)

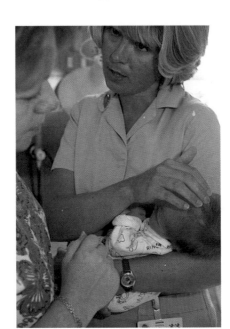

Midwives offer support to mothers before and after the birth

- giving advice about such matters as immunisation (injections).

As funds become tighter, fewer school nurses are being employed.

Community psychiatric nurses

Community psychiatric nurses (CPNs) and the community-based mental handicap nurses (RNMHs) provide continuing care and support for people who have been receiving long-term hospital care and who have now returned to living in the community.

The link between health and social care is through social workers and community-based nurses.

Radiographers

There are two types of radiographer. Diagnostic radiographers use X-rays and ultrasound to check internal organs for abnormalities. Therapeutic radiographers use ionising radiation (such as X-rays and gamma rays) to destroy tissues in the treatment of patients. Therapeutic radiography is used on a wide range of cancers.

The radiographer works as a technician supporting the radiologist. The radiologist is a specialist doctor who, for example, interprets X-ray pictures and produces reports for the doctor requesting the X-ray.

? What are the main differences between the job of a hospital doctor and a hospital nurse?

Think
IT THROUGH

Physiotherapists

Physiotherapists have an important role to play in improving the mobility and health of patients using supportive and manipulative exercises. They often use equipment such as infrared and ultrasound machines.

Physiotherapists work in co-operation with doctors in planning physiotherapy programmes.

There are now approximately 9500 physiotherapists working in the NHS in the UK. A number work in private practice.

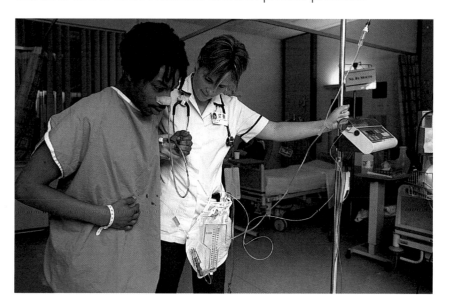

A physiotherapist at work

Occupational therapists

Occupational therapists (known as OTs) work in the NHS to treat illness, both mental and physical, with activity. A large part of their work is with clients or patients suffering from a physical or learning difficulty.

OTs work on a one-to-one basis, with groups and with recreational activities, with an aim of rehabilitating clients (this means *helping people to cope with daily living*) and teaching them basic living skills.

Many OTs work in the community and are also employed by Social Service Departments offering advice on aids and adaptations to daily living.

Many OTs work in the community

Speech therapists

Speech therapists help people with speech disorders. These range from children with delayed speech development to older people recovering from strokes. Most of their work is with children.

Chiropodists

Chiropodists work on the feet of people in all client groups. They deal with such complaints as:

- corns
- ingrown toenails
- hammer toes.

Find out what these conditions are if you don't already know.

Over 1 million chiropody sessions are carried out each year and the majority of people who receive this service are 65 or over.

Social workers

Social workers can be divided into:

- community care workers
- residential care workers
- domiciliary and day care workers.

Working in all these areas are qualified social workers who have obtained a qualification covering all areas of social work, although they may specialise in one area later. The qualification most social workers hold today is the Diploma in Social Work (Dip SW).

Social workers provide support to all types of clients, individuals and families, both in the community or in hospitals (where they are known as hospital social workers).

Many provide social rehabilitation and community services, specialising in child care work, helping older people or working with people suffering from mental illness.

The role of the social worker is to:

- assess a client's and carer's needs and
- organise services, with other professionals, to meet those individual needs.

Home carers

Home carers provide emotional, social and practical support to clients living in their own home in the community.

Local authorities have a duty (this means they must provide this service) to provide home care assistants or home carers (who used to be known as home helps).

Many home care assistants work for private organisations and offer people a service in their own home for a fee. The private sector provided 44 per cent of home care services in 2001 as compared to just 2 per cent in 1992.

A home carer can help people to stay in their own home for as long as they wish

Working mostly with older people, home carers carry out such tasks as simple cleaning, lighting fires, shopping, cooking and basic personal tasks. They also write letters and provide social support (this really means *company*). Home carers also work with people with physical disabilities and families with young children who are in need.

Meals-on-wheels staff

This service is becoming increasingly important as more and more older dependent people choose to live in their own home. This service is provided by the local authority in many areas, but it is still also offered by voluntary agencies such as the Women's Royal Voluntary Service or the Women's Institute in rural areas. The private sector (this means *commercial enterprises*) now provides 41 per cent of meals delivered to people in their own homes and 65 per cent of meals to luncheon clubs.

Meals-on-wheels can make an important contribution to nutritional needs

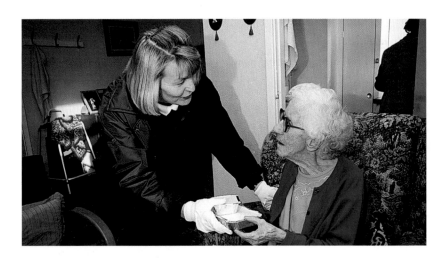

Meals-on-wheels is one of the most important forms of community support for older people in their own home. It makes a contribution to their nutritional needs and is often the only social contact that an older person has during the week. The service can also improve the morale of older people. As older people are most susceptible to hypothermia (this means *abnormally low body temperature*) when the weather is cold, the daily visit of meals-on-wheels staff can provide a chance to check that all is well.

FIND IT OUT

Find out what 'morale' means.

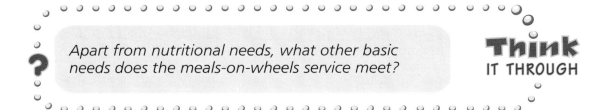

Think
IT THROUGH

Apart from nutritional needs, what other basic needs does the meals-on-wheels service meet?

Skills needed by care professionals

You have probably chosen to do a course in health and social care because you are interested in people. You may be the sort of person friends contact to talk over problems. You may have appreciated someone else listening to you to help you out. Your interest in helping people is a great advantage in health and social care situations when you may be expected to give clients support. You may be able to think of examples when you have been in hospital or any other unfamiliar situation yourself, and been glad of someone's warmth and friendliness towards you.

Just as people have **physical needs,** such as the need for food, sleep and warmth, and it is necessary to satisfy these needs, they also have **emotional needs,** such as the need to be liked, to be loved, to be wanted and respected or to be thought special.

Often physical needs are direct, easy to see and in many cases easy to satisfy.

Emotional needs, however, are more tricky to see and to satisfy. And perhaps because these needs are less obvious and more difficult, carers can become preoccupied with physical tasks and fail to pick up on emotional needs. It is important to try not to fall into the trap of providing physical care only. Remember, people have feelings, and feelings matter.

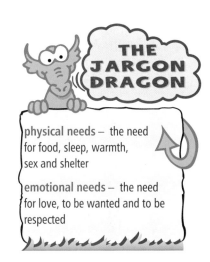

THE JARGON DRAGON

physical needs – the need for food, sleep, warmth, sex and shelter

emotional needs – the need for love, to be wanted and to be respected

The importance of communication
The fact that it is extremely difficult *not* to communicate shows how important communication is. For a fun experiment, see how long you can manage without communication!

Think
IT THROUGH

In your group, discuss how hard it must be for prisoners held in solitary confinement.

Our instinct is to communicate with others because relationships hinge on communication, and without relationships living would be mere existence.

We tend to think of communication as speaking, but there are many ways to impart meaning or messages to others. It isn't just what we say that creates impressions, but also how we express the words, what we wear, how we stand, look, behave, listen and respond.

People have an instinct to communicate and develop relationships

Communication is important because it helps us to:

- live our lives *practically*
- develop *psychologically and intellectually*
- express ourselves *emotionally*
- form relationships *socially*.

Effective communication skills

There are a number of techniques you can practise that will help you to communicate effectively with other people. You can practise:

- taking opportunities to start conversations
- observing
- listening actively and reflectively
- showing empathy (this means *identifying completely with another person*)
- knowing when to keep quiet

- knowing how to 'read' and use non-verbal communication, such as facial expressions, use of eye contact and posture
- knowing how to ask questions
- respecting people as individuals
- listening to others' point of view.

Think
IT THROUGH

Think of some examples of someone 'communicating effectively' with you. How did they achieve a successful result? Discuss your examples in class.

The effectiveness of your communication skills may depend on how far your approach meets the needs of the other person. For example, you will have to approach a 3-year-old child differently from the way you approach your tutor. Language, posture, pace and tone all need to be adapted to the other person.

The psychologist Maslow suggested that people have a 'hierarchy of needs'. This hierarchy (this means *grading system*) starts with very basic biological needs, such as food, warmth and going to the toilet, and goes right up to more complex psychological needs. It is only when the basic needs have been met that it becomes possible to work on fulfilling other needs.

Non-verbal communication

A large part of communication is actually carried out without speaking. This is called non-verbal communication or body language.

Smiling – One of the most significant forms of non-verbal communication is a smile. Smiling shows warmth and openness, and helps your interactions (this means *two-way talking*) to be positive.

Eye contact – Eye contact is one of the most direct ways of communicating. For example, many of you will have received or made romantic intentions clear without speaking a word!

Where you focus your eyes makes a difference to the interaction you achieve. The length of your gaze also makes a difference. It is not a good idea to stare clients out, but it is necessary to look at them so that they know they have your attention.

Eye contact is one of the most direct ways of communicating

Think IT THROUGH

You need to be aware of your own usual facial expression. This can affect how you communicate. If you know the people in your group well it may be useful to go round and say how each member of the group usually appears. Some people look permanently worried or unhappy, when they are not at all, but that is the way they come across.

Posture – Think whether your body language conveys messages like 'Yes, I am listening. I want to hear what you say' or 'No, I'm eager to leave. I'm not interested.' Sitting beside the person you are talking to, without distractions or barriers like desks separating you, makes the difference between good and poor communication patterns. Stretching back in your chair away from the person you are talking to sends messages of distance and carelessness, while leaning forward nodding, saying 'yes' or making quiet utterances reinforces your interest to the client.

Stretching back in your chair may indicate lack of concern . . .

CONNECT COUNSELLING SERVICES

Gestures – Think about how you use your hands in communication. Drumming fingers implies impatience, as might jangling your keys in your pocket or twiddling your thumbs. Sometimes people use their hands to cover their faces and this may imply they have something to hide – they are being defensive

Touch – Touch or physical contact is a very tricky aspect of non-verbal communication and needs some confidence in its use. Occasionally a hand on someone's shoulder or arm can be very reassuring and giving a distressed child a hug after a bad fall can be a spontaneous response.

The issue of physical contact can easily be misunderstood or misrepresented if it is described to someone else in the wrong way. This is particularly true if different genders are involved, for example in the case of a male nursery nurse working with children. This means your actions must always be above any criticism. It is best to ensure other staff are around if physical contact occurs.

Space/distance – Have you ever noticed how people stand a safe distance apart when they don't know each other? Have you ever felt uncomfortable when somebody you don't know has edged on to your side of the seat on a train or a bus? Some people stand very close to you when they talk and it makes you feel uneasy.

THE JARGON DRAGON

personal space – the space that people need for themselves where only those they know well can enter

Everyone has their own '**personal space**'. That is the space that they need for themselves where only those they know well can enter. When people are compelled to be near each other for some reason, in a lift, for example, they often adopt little mechanisms to avoid catching the eye of other people, such as staring at the floor or concentrating on a book.

How poor communication skills may reduce the effectiveness of care

Try to improve your listening and questioning skills, and be conscious of your body language to improve the effectiveness of your care. Other physical or practical factors, such as noise or interruptions, or barriers like desks or chairs, may spoil or stop good interaction with the other person. Sometimes the room temperature may be so cold or so hot that it is difficult to concentrate on the matter in hand. You or the client may be very tired or hungry. Children and many adults find it hard to take in what is being said if they are tired, thirsty or hungry.

As well as physical barriers affecting your rapport with the other person, there may be language problems or a speech difficulty, which will slow down the interaction.

There will be also many occasions when the other person finds it difficult to talk because of emotional factors, such as anger, shame or great sadness.

The values that underpin all care work with clients

Personal values and attitudes

Much of our interpersonal (this means *between people*) interaction is guided by our personal values and attitudes. In other words, what we think is right and true affects the way we behave. Many of the ideas and assumptions we have are based on what we were told as children and later on what we have seen and heard on television or read about. Sometimes our own prejudices or personal fears and values are more subtle, but are still significant in affecting how we relate to people.

Care values

Care values are principles, standards or qualities considered worthwhile or desirable by the care profession. It is possible to tell by their behaviour what an individual's attitudes and values are, such as whether they have sexist or racist views. (You will find out more about attitudes and behaviour later on in this section.) Although it is difficult to change attitudes, if you work in the health and social care field it is important to pay them a great deal of attention. Care values to think about include the following:

- anti-discriminatory practice – not judging people because of their culture, race, religion, sexual identity, age, gender, health status, etc.
- confidentiality – clients have the right to say who should have access to their personal information and care workers are responsible for respecting the wishes of the client
- individual rights and choice – clients' choices, preferences and wishes must be respected
- personal beliefs and identity – each individual's own personal religious, cultural, political, ethical and sexual beliefs and preferences must be respected
- effective communication – listening to other individuals, promoting effective communication in a variety of ways, considering language (verbal and non-verbal), understanding, environment, and social and cultural influences.

All these issues are known together as the care value base. It is hoped that by stimulating thought and discussion through training and exposing carers to a wide variety of situations, attitudes may be developed that are consistent with this value base.

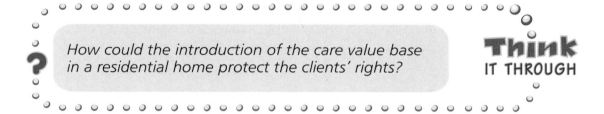

How could the introduction of the care value base in a residential home protect the clients' rights?

Think
IT THROUGH

Protecting individuals from abuse

The intention of having care values is to create equality (this means *the same conditions*) for all individuals. Most professional carers are employed by agencies that have considerable power, and also have responsibilities in law to others besides the clients, who are also known as service users. While the supportive and counselling roles of care workers are emphasised here, care workers are also responsible to the agency that they work for. Care workers may possess more power, through their position, than their clients. To guard against any difficulties that may arise because of these power imbalances care workers should:

- *identify* and question their own values and prejudices, and their implications for practice
- *respect* and value uniqueness and diversity, and recognise and build on strengths
- *promote* people's rights to choice, privacy, confidentiality and protection, while recognising and addressing the complexities of competing rights and demands
- *assist* people to increase control of their life and improve quality, while recognising that control of behaviour will be required at times in order to protect children and adults from harm
- *identify*, analyse and take action to counter discrimination, racism, disadvantage, inequality and injustice, using strategies appropriate to the situation
- *practise* in a manner that does not stigmatise or disadvantage either individuals, groups or communities.

THE JARGON DRAGON

socialisation – the process whereby people become members of their society and learn its rules

The social or health problems of some clients may create real dependency, where they come to rely almost totally on other people to meet their needs. To be perceived (this means *seen*) as anything other than fit, able and making a valuable contribution to society is to be stripped of power. Those who provide care services may well show the attitudes of the society into which they themselves have been socialised. They may have attitudes that reinforce many of the prejudices that society has about people who are different, for whatever reason.

Confidentiality

Confidentiality is a principle common to all health, social care and early years services. This means that before any information you have about a client is shared with other people the client's permission must be obtained. If the reasons why you want to share the information are made clear to the client, then consent is more likely to be given.

If someone trusts you sufficiently to talk to you deeply about themselves or their problems, this trust should never be broken. It is demeaning and disrespectful to the other person if you chat about them openly. It would also be very distressing to anyone who knew the other person. If you need help yourself because of what the client has told you, you must go to the supervisor in private.

There are two levels of confidentiality. At the first level there are many things about which you need never speak to anyone. If it is your task on placement to help an older man who has wet himself to change his trousers, you do the task and say nothing about it. It is unprofessional to moan to your friends on the way home on the bus about what a fuss it was. Think about a time when you found yourself in an embarrassing situation. How did you feel?

At the second level, if someone is discussing an issue with you and you feel that what they say will cut across legal boundaries or the rules of the establishment you are in, then you will have to warn them of that, and pass the information on. For example, if someone was about to tell you in a hostel that they sniffed glue, then you would have to say that you need to speak to someone more senior. If they had already told you, then the same rule would apply.

There are certain times when client confidentiality has to be limited:

- if the client is a danger to themselves or others
- if they are unconscious and cannot give information about their medical condition
- if they are about to commit or have committed crimes
- if a court of law requests information
- if any kind of abuse has taken or is about to take place.

Individual rights

Unless you treat each person as an individual you are likely to make assumptions about them – that is make a judgement about them based on something you have seen or read. The judgement may be wrong but it still affects your interaction with that person. The assumption grows to a stereotype. This means that we make the person fit the image we have of them rather than accepting them for what they are. Stereotypes act as barriers to good communication. You will find more on ways of avoiding acting on stereotypes in the section on anti-discriminatory practice on pages 59–63.

Good carers try to be aware of the stereotypes they may create, particularly when the person they are trying to help is from a different social class background, a different ethnic (this means *racial*) background or is of the opposite gender. Here are some examples of how we can easily misjudge people and get the wrong message.

Gender
We are socialised into our gender roles from the minute we are born, by the colour of the blanket that is wrapped around us and the sort of cards that are sent to greet our arrival.

Ask your parents what colour clothes they would buy for a boy or girl baby.

FIND IT OUT

Age

When did you last run a marathon? It is not only older people who do not normally run marathons. Negative stereotyping about age highlights sickness, dependency and not being able to be sociable. Older people may be seen by others as retarded, slow or inefficient. If they show interest in sexual matters this may be regarded as odd, funny or dirty.

Disability

Often assumptions are made about disabled people's abilities based on misunderstanding. Access and opportunities are very significant to disabled people. If they are denied access to a building or the opportunity to do a job then they cannot demonstrate the abilities they have. Some disabled people with mobility difficulties have been denied access to nightclubs and other venues, supposedly because they pose a fire risk.

Acknowledging an individual's personal belief and identity

The possible effects of discrimination are so pervasive and wide-ranging that it is impossible to explain or describe them in depth or with accuracy. Reading novels, poems, watching films or television programmes and listening to personal experiences can help you to learn about the possible effects of discrimination.

Think
IT THROUGH

Consider the physical, intellectual, emotional and social implications of discrimination for the following groups:

- *women*
- *ethnic minority group members*
- *disabled people.*

Everyone stereotypes to a certain extent. We create judgements about people in our mind so that we can interact with them. For example, if you met a young man wearing sporty clothes you might assume he enjoyed playing sport. If you met a teenage girl wearing trendy clothes you might assume she liked listening to music and socialising. You might be very wrong in both cases, but such misjudgements are probably not damaging.

However, stereotyping can be damaging and can become discrimination. It is not easy to say at exactly what point this happens, because there may only be a subtle difference between stereotyping being helpful or being damaging to the other person. If you divide people into different categories you cannot assume that people who look or behave in a way that matches an image you have in your mind will fit into a set category.

When people make assumptions like this it is described as prejudice. It means someone has prejudged the other person or group, or made up their minds beforehand. They have a personal bias, based on something they have heard or seen. It is confirmed and perpetuated (this means *carried on*) in their response to people and their interactions with them.

Look at the comments below – you will see that there is prejudice and unhelpful categorisation in them:

- A woman's place is in the home.
- People with AIDS have got what they deserve.
- People with disabilities shouldn't have children – it's not fair to the children.
- Lesbians and gays shouldn't teach in schools.

Anti-discriminatory practice/ non-discriminatory attitude

While prejudice is what a person thinks, discrimination is what a person does. **Discrimination** describes how one person treats another person or group unfairly, based on their prejudice.

Forms of discrimination
Visual clues – Visual clues often guide our first impressions. We make judgements about people based on what we see.

THE JARGON DRAGON

discrimination – what a person does to treat another person or group unfairly, based on prejudice

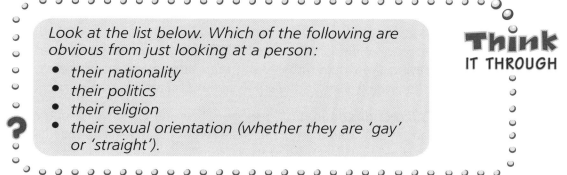

Look at the list below. Which of the following are obvious from just looking at a person:

- *their nationality*
- *their politics*
- *their religion*
- *their sexual orientation (whether they are 'gay' or 'straight').*

Think
IT THROUGH

Language – There are many sexist and racist terms in our language, which are indirectly discriminatory. For example, often the words 'man', 'he' and 'him' are used to refer to both genders. This can be seen as excluding women.

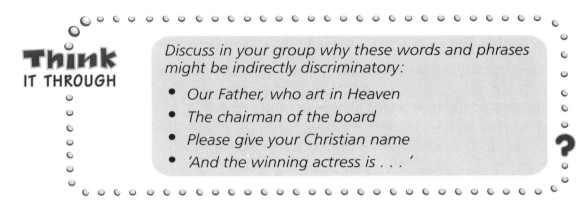

Think
IT THROUGH

Discuss in your group why these words and phrases might be indirectly discriminatory:

- *Our Father, who art in Heaven*
- *The chairman of the board*
- *Please give your Christian name*
- *'And the winning actress is . . . '*

Levels of discrimination

Discrimination can arise at several levels:

- An individual level, where people may have personal attitudes and beliefs that they use to prejudge other groups negatively.

- An institutional level, where the systems and practices of an organisation exclude certain groups from access to resources. For example, if publicity about antenatal classes was not produced in community languages (such as Punjabi or Urdu) in a multi-racial area, this could be seen as 'institutional racism'.

- A cultural level, where people have absorbed values, beliefs and ideas so deeply that they don't challenge negative stereotypes in media images. These people accept racist or sexist remarks without question.

Direct and indirect discrimination

THE
JARGON
DRAGON

direct discrimination –
blatantly treating people less favourably than others because of their gender, race or disability etc.

indirect discrimination –
where conditions are set that exclude certain groups because of their sex, race, gender etc.

Direct discrimination is behaviour that is blatantly prejudiced. This includes using offensive language, denying people rights or being rude. For example, a young black girl was sitting on the inside seat of a bus. Her white friend sitting beside her stood up to let an older woman sit down. The woman refused the seat saying she would rather stand than sit next to 'one of them'. That young black girl was the victim of direct discrimination.

Indirect discrimination is more subtle and less easy to report, but equally damaging. The male senior manager who may have decided he doesn't want to promote a female assistant manager may find ways of undermining the female assistant's confidence (giving her menial and tedious jobs to do or always commenting that she is not competent), so that she doesn't even feel she can apply for the post. She becomes the victim of indirect discrimination.

Devaluing someone by not taking them seriously or not respecting what they say is a form of indirect discrimination. For example, assuming that everyone has a Christian name is a form of indirect discrimination, since not everyone is a Christian and may be named in a different way.

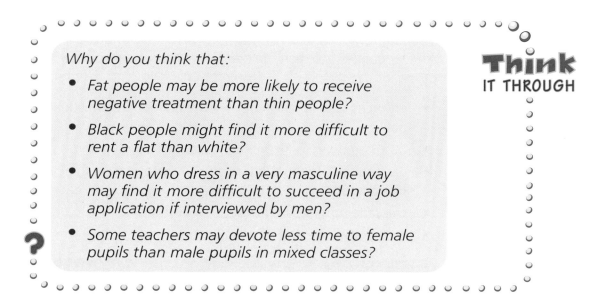

Why do you think that:

- *Fat people may be more likely to receive negative treatment than thin people?*

- *Black people might find it more difficult to rent a flat than white?*

- *Women who dress in a very masculine way may find it more difficult to succeed in a job application if interviewed by men?*

- *Some teachers may devote less time to female pupils than male pupils in mixed classes?*

Think IT THROUGH

Racial discrimination

It is easy for black people or minority groups to be nudged out of health care services and therefore discriminated against almost without people noticing. Similarly, in schools, attitudes are set and may create tensions before any learning takes place. In the community people are worried about rising unemployment and house prices, and these fears are often taken out on minority groups. Securing housing and employment therefore becomes more problematic for black people and, coupled with potential educational difficulties, such groups become disadvantaged through discrimination.

The Commission for Racial Equality has been set up to help with such problems. It:

- carries out formal investigations
- decides if discrimination has taken place after investigation
- produces reports on its investigations
- makes recommendations as to action following investigations
- publishes examples of good practice and gives advice.

Think IT THROUGH

What things could a manager of a residential home do to make sure that discrimination does not occur at the home?

?

Sexual discrimination

Some research shows that more people actually want to have boy rather than girl babies. Why do you think this may be true?

The Equal Opportunities Commission was set up to deal with inequalities between the genders in the workplace and outside. It:

- enforces laws in respect of sex discrimination and equal pay
- has the power to investigate cases of discrimination
- can require organisations to provide information to any investigation
- can take up cases on behalf of individuals
- provides advice and information.

FIND IT OUT

Find out what the Equal Opportunities Commission does. Look at their website, www.eoc.org.uk

Discrimination and disability

Many disabled people feel that one of the worst aspects of being disabled is the way other people perceive them. Very often it is assumed that disabled people cannot do things. For example, if someone is in a wheelchair many people address the person pushing the wheelchair rather than the person in the wheelchair. Of course, it is naive to suggest that a disabled person can do everything despite their disability, but if appropriate access, services and support are provided new opportunities can be opened up. There is also a lot of evidence of disabled people achieving physical and academic feats that some able-bodied people would never dream of.

Since 1970 all public buildings must by law provide wheelchair access. Similarly, pathways, walkways and staircases should not restrict wheelchair users. In reality, there are still enormous difficulties in terms of access. This limits disabled people socially and in connection with employment. It is a similar story with housing. If a disabled person has an adapted home, which they can manage, this increases their independence. If funds are low and they have to rely on other people then they remain limited.

The Disability Rights Commission was set up to promote the rights of disabled people and works to eliminate discrimination against disabled people. It:

- encourages good practice to eliminate discrimination
- checks up on the working of the Disability Discrimination Act 1995
- advises the government about disability matters.

Protecting people from prejudice

Most people have preferences. It is helpful if you are aware of your own preferences so that you can work on them to prevent prejudice developing. When you make decisions or choices you must try to avoid your own personal bias or preference affecting your judgements. This is particularly important when you are out on work placement. It is easy to prefer the attractive, well-dressed infant at the local school and to assume they are more intelligent than some of the others and treat them accordingly. Some of the less attractive pupils may be equally or more capable, however, and deserve recognition.

People tend to categorise on sight or first impressions and research shows that:

- fat people are more likely to get negative treatment
- in mixed classes teachers devote more time to male pupils than to female
- women who dress in a very masculine way are less likely to succeed in a job application if interviewed by men
- supervisors sum up young workers' behaviour in the first couple of weeks and don't change their opinions.

Protecting children

If you are working with young children you can try to counteract stereotypical practices and language by:

- encouraging role reversal – let the boys play in the home corner and the girls with Lego
- selecting books and posters reflecting positive images of black children and non-sexist attitudes

- presenting toys and equipment in a non-sexist way

- avoiding sexist, racist language yourself, but also monitoring children's conversations

- being firm about any discriminatory actions or language from children – act quickly to report it to a member of staff if you don't feel that it is appropriate for you to deal with it

- never saying things like 'Big boys don't cry' – it's OK for any child to have a good bawl, male or female

- not separating children on the basis of gender – use birth dates or names with particular letters

- pointing out good role models, such as a female garage hand, a female doctor or a male nurse.

Protecting people at work

Most establishments have equal opportunities policies and codes of practice for dealing with racist remarks, attitudes or actions. Make sure you know whom to report to if you see or hear anything you regard as racist or sexist. If matters are dealt with promptly it is less likely that feelings will run high and escalate into violence.

Legislation relating to discrimination

The Race Relations Act 1976

This Act made racial discrimination illegal in public life. It says people can take action on matters like employment, housing, education and provision of goods and services.

The Act covers:

- direct discrimination – treating a person less favourably on the grounds of race
- indirect discrimination – applying certain criteria that work to the disadvantage of one person over another.

It also makes victimisation illegal. This means it is against the law to treat somebody unfairly for being involved in making a complaint about discrimination.

The Commission for Racial Equality can help in the preparation of Race Relations Act cases. The Citizens' Advice Bureau can also assist with these matters.

The Race Relations (Amendment) Act 2000

This amendment Act:

- extends protection by increasing the responsibilities of public authorities
- makes police chief constables liable for any discrimination by their officers
- places new responsibilities on small employers not to discriminate
- states that people must not discriminate when selling, letting or managing property.

The Chronically Sick and Disabled Persons Act 1970

This Act attempted to reduce discrimination against disabled people. It instructed local authorities to provide services for disabled people and legislated (this means *made it law*) that any new public buildings must provide access for disabled people.

The services that the Act recommended should be available to disabled people include:

- home care workers (used to be called home helps)
- meals-on-wheels
- adaptations to homes
- telephones
- aids to daily living
- occupation at home and at centres
- outings
- provision of transport.

The Act stated that local authorities had to know how many disabled people there were living in their area.

The National Health Service Act 1977

This Act went on to make it a duty of the local authority to provide some home help services and recommended the provision of services of washing clothes for people who need them.

The Disabled Persons Act 1986 (Services, Consultation and Representation)

This Act reinforced the need for assessment for disabled people and services. A disabled person or their representative may request an assessment. This means they have the right to ask to have the level of their disability and their needs looked at and reported on by an expert.

The Sex Discrimination Act 1975

The Act applies to men and women. It states that it is unlawful to discriminate in the employment areas of recruitment, selection, promotion and training. It is also unlawful to treat a person less favourably because they are married. Like the Race Relations Act, it includes direct and indirect discrimination as well as victimisation.

The Equal Opportunities Commission and the Citizens' Advice Bureau can assist with complaints.

Equal Pay Act 1970 (amended 1983)

This Act should be considered alongside the Sex Discrimination Act. The main point of the Act is that equal work must be rewarded with equal pay regardless of gender.

Fair Employment Act 1989

In Northern Ireland the Fair Employment Act 1989 covers the area of religious discrimination. There is no legislation relating to religious discrimination in England and Wales (2002).

Disabled Persons Acts 1944 and 1988

Both Acts obliged companies employing more than 20 staff to employ 3 per cent disabled people.

Employment Protection Act 1978

This Act consisted of rights to guarantee pay, time off work, maternity rights (this means *for women during pregnancy and after childbirth*), sick pay and access to computerised data about the employee. Trade unions could be recognised at the discretion of the employer. Recognised unions can insist on equal opportunities policies and analysis of data to show how many black and white, male and female, disabled and non-disabled workers are employed by the company.

The Disability Discrimination Act 1995

This Act introduced new rights for people with disabilities in employment, transport, education and access to goods and services. Employers with 20 or more employees are required to treat people with a disability no less favourably than any other employee. Employers have to provide facilities to allow people with disabilities to be employed in the workplace.

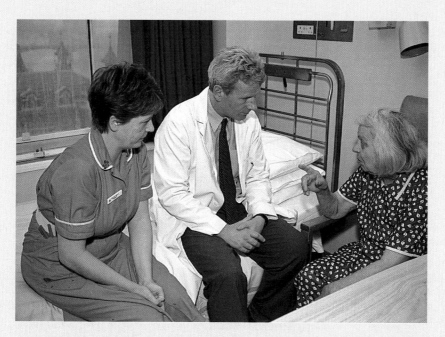

Mrs Poole is 86. She is independent but has suffered a stroke at home. She was found by a friend who called an ambulance and she was admitted to hospital.

After she had been in hospital for a week the hospital social worker called a meeting of all the people who were looking after her. At the meeting were the doctor, nurses, dietician, physiotherapist and also, most important of all, Mrs Poole herself.

It was hoped that she would go into a residential home but Mrs Poole felt strongly that she wanted to go back to her own home, although the doctor and rest of the team did not agree. However Mrs Poole's wishes had to be taken into account and it was agreed to organise community services to help her live as independent a life as possible in her own home.

It was agreed that she would receive the following:

- meals-on-wheels seven days a week, until she could cook her own meals again

- support from the community/district nurse

- a carer to bath her four times a week

- a home carer to cook her breakfast and evening meals

- support from the occupational therapist to show her how to look after herself again.

case study

Mrs Poole

After about six months a second meeting was called by the social worker, as Mrs Poole's health had got worse. Mrs Poole agreed to enter a residential home. She visited a number of establishments before deciding on one she liked. When she was admitted to the home she was encouraged to stay registered with the same doctor and to keep in touch with her friends.

Q *Describe the methods of referral used in the case study.*

Explain the role of all the professionals in the case meeting.

What was Mrs Poole's role in the case meeting?

Which elements of the care value base have been met in the case study?

Describe how the workers in this case empowered Mrs Poole.

This unit will help you to:

look after your own health and well-being and to understand ways of promoting health and well-being for others.

In this unit you will learn about:

Understanding health and well-being

Everyone wants to be healthy. It is easy to take being healthy for granted, until something goes wrong and we become ill.

'Health' comes from an Old English word meaning 'whole', and the term includes physical, emotional, intellectual and social well-being. Health and well-being should mean that a person feels positively well and is not just free of disease or illness. It is difficult to define and collect information about 'well-being', as it often relates to how individual people feel about themselves and their personal experiences. Well-being is harder to define than illness, as it is often taken for granted. To make it clearer, there are three ways of looking at health and well-being:

- A negative way of looking at health and well-being can be to look at it as the absence of any physical illness, disease or mental distress. This definition is saying that a person has done nothing to contribute to this healthy state.
- A more positive way of looking at health and well-being is to say that a person achieves a healthy state through becoming and staying physically fit and mentally healthy. This means that the person contributes to their own well-being through keeping healthy and fit.
- The 'holistic way' of looking at health and well-being is when physical, social, intellectual and emotional factors are all seen to contribute to the health of the individual.

Think
IT THROUGH

In groups, discuss what it means to be healthy. Agree on a definition of health and well-being.

People's basic health needs do not change. The differences are in the ability of each person to provide for his or her own needs. In other words, people need different amounts and types of support to meet their needs throughout life.

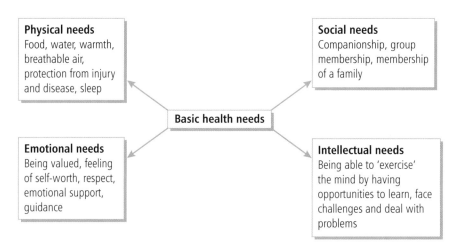

Physical needs
Food, water, warmth, breathable air, protection from injury and disease, sleep

Social needs
Companionship, group membership, membership of a family

Basic health needs

Emotional needs
Being valued, feeling of self-worth, respect, emotional support, guidance

Intellectual needs
Being able to 'exercise' the mind by having opportunities to learn, face challenges and deal with problems

Basic health needs of individuals

Different needs also have differing importance:

- Food, water and shelter – **basic human physical needs** – are essential to stay alive.
- The next most important need is safety.
- Having achieved the first two needs, a person is in need of emotional and social support.
- Only when all these needs have been met is it realistic to consider needs for self-respect and **self-esteem** and, finally, personal fulfilment.

For example, people who are starving may take risks, which could affect their health and well-being, or may be prepared to degrade themselves by doing things they would not do if they were fully fed. The primary need of starving people is for food and only later can they consider their own self-respect.

THE JARGON DRAGON

basic human physical needs – needs of humans that must be met in order for them to stay alive, namely food, shelter, warmth and water

self esteem – how people value themselves

What basic physical needs do these children have?

lifestyle factors – causes of health problems, including diet, age, exercise and sleep

In addition to these factors, increasing attention is being paid to **lifestyle factors**. Why do cancer, heart disease and stroke occur most commonly in Western society? The quest for finding out is known as **epidemiology**. Epidemiologists are now identifying lifestyle factors, particularly diet and lack of exercise, as causes of health problems. We all therefore have the power to influence our own health and that of our family.

Think
IT THROUGH

Jenny, who is 45, has been healthy all her life. She has never had any serious illness. What definition of health and well-being would you apply to her situation?

Basic needs essential to health and well-being at different life stages

Life stage	Basic health need	How the need is expressed and met
Child 0–2	Physical	Food, warmth and water from parents. Medical support/vaccination for long-term protection
	Social	Very solitary, relying on carers, brothers and sisters for social roles
	Emotional	Very reliant on primary carers for emotional support
	Intellectual	Learning to play and learn from new situations
2–10	Physical	Walking gives access to a range of areas. Food and warmth and protection from carers
	Social	Developing circle of friends. Greater range of social contacts
	Emotional	Very reliant on primary carers for emotional support and as models for beliefs
	Intellectual	Learning through play. Formal education
Adolescent 10-18	Physical	Rapid growth at puberty linked to taking more personal control of supplying physical needs

Life stage	Basic health need	How the need is expressed and met
10–18 cont.	Social	Peer group (people of same age and interests) becomes very important. Group membership provides support beyond the family
	Emotional	A time of mixed emotions needing careful support. Starts to move away from parents to peers for support
	Intellectual	Formal education. More learning from experience as new situations are met in peer groups
Adult 18–65	Physical	Becoming self-reliant and a provider of physical support for others (becoming a parent)
	Social	Develops through a variety of stages including marriage, starting a family and children leaving home
	Emotional	Developing strong attachments to a partner. Being a model for and supplying support for others in family
	Intellectual	Formal education reduces. Challenges come from work and family roles
Older adult 65+	Physical	Senses become less efficient. General wear and tear means support from others or artificial aids (e.g. spectacles) may be needed
	Social	Family will have left home. One partner may die before the other. Movement difficulties increase isolation. Organised activities support social well-being
	Emotional	Friends and relatives get older and die. Children become independent, so emotional support needs to come from other people. Often a time where reduced ability means self-esteem and self-worth are low
	Intellectual	Mental activity often outstrips physical ability, leading to some frustration. Intellectual stimuli are very important

Positive and negative influences on health and well-being

Here are some positive factors that affect your health:

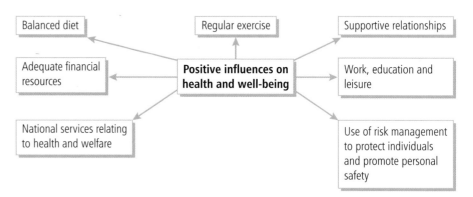

A balanced diet

Different people need different amounts of energy in the form of food each day. The amount of energy needed depends on age, sex, size and activity level. People with high energy needs, such as children, manual workers and teenagers, will need to take in more energy than less active people. People who do not do much exercise may need to cut down on high energy foods.

Benefits of a balanced diet

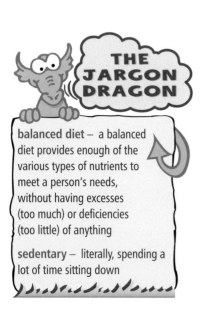

THE JARGON DRAGON

balanced diet – a balanced diet provides enough of the various types of nutrients to meet a person's needs, without having excesses (too much) or deficiencies (too little) of anything

sedentary – literally, spending a lot of time sitting down

If you are eating a balanced diet:

- it will be matched to your needs (if you are in hot climate you will eat lighter foods than in a cold climate; if you have a **sedentary** job in an office you have different food needs than someone doing heavy manual work)
- your weight should be correct for your height (see chart on page 123)
- it will help prevent disease as all your the body systems should be in balance.

FIND
IT
OUT

Does an assistant working in a shop need to eat the same diet as a worker in a coal-mine?

Young children

All human beings need nutrients (for example, protein and vitamins such as thiamin and calcium) to support growth and maintain health. For some groups of people, such as children, this is particularly important. Some children may find it difficult to eat well, if they are ill, upset or worried about something, or if they have a condition that means they cannot eat certain types of food. Religious or other strong beliefs held by their parents may also affect what they eat.

THE JARGON DRAGON

protein – a nutrient found in many foods, from meat and dairy products to vegetables and fruit, which helps build and repair cells and tissues in the body

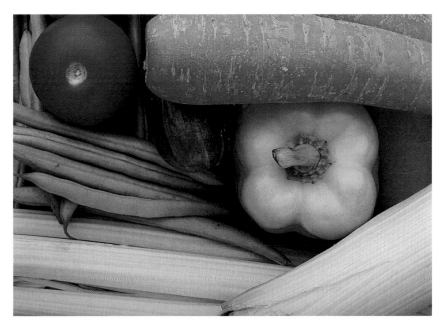

Vegetables play an inportant part in a balanced, healthy diet

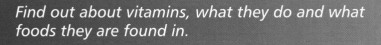

Find out about vitamins, what they do and what foods they are found in.

FIND
IT
OUT

Adolescents

Adolescents also have high nutritional needs. They may find it difficult to eat balanced meals because they are busy or because they may not care to sit down to family meals. They may skip meals because what they are doing is too exciting to stop to eat.

Is fast food, such as burgers, good for you?

Adolescents are also becoming aware of their body shape and may want to lose or put on weight. This is a vulnerable time for developing eating disorders like anorexia (starving oneself) and bulimia (binge eating followed by vomiting or taking laxatives). Young people are often influenced by media images of what they should eat, what they should drink and how they should appear. Emotionally, adolescence can be a turbulent time and eating can also be an escape or a comfort at a time of pressures over exams, career choices, parents and relationships.

Think
IT THROUGH

Look at the advertisements in a women's magazine for clothes, make-up etc. Why do you think that all the models in the advertisements are slim?

Janice is a very sensible girl of 15, who loves her active social life. She has very strong feelings about her appearance. She keeps an eye on her weight and makes sure that it is normal for her age and height. She goes to exercise classes twice a week and has made good friends there. She likes socialising at the weekends.

Janice has a very good friend called Joanne. Janice is very worried about Joanne because she wants to look like some of the very thin pop singers. Joanne is very particular about what she eats, and is very underweight for her height and age. She does no exercise but enjoys socialising in the evenings. She is beginning to feel tired and has difficulty sleeping. She is falling behind with her school work.

Q *Why do you think Joanne wishes to look like she does?*

Which of the two girls do you think might have the highest self-esteem?

What are the social benefits to Janice of her exercise classes?

Many young people eat too little because they want to look like 'glamorous' media stars

Adults

The cost of food and the time it takes to prepare meals may be of concern to adults. This is particularly the case if they work and have family responsibilities, and if they are on a low income.

Sometimes people fail to eat well because they are anxious or stressed about relationships, family and work problems or lack of work. These situations can also cause people to overeat for comfort.

Think
IT THROUGH

There are many reasons why people overeat or become overweight. Come up with a list of possible reasons after discussion in class. Some examples might be decreased mobility in older people and the calorie levels in alcohol.

?

Pregnant women and breast-feeding mothers

Pregnant women and women who are breast-feeding need a high intake of protein, iron, calcium, folic acid (a B-group vitamin) and vitamins C and D. Sometimes mineral and vitamin supplements are prescribed by the doctor, but is also important to have a good diet, so that the body gets these elements naturally.

Healthy eating is especially important for expectant and nursing mothers

Older people

Older people may have lower energy requirements because of decreased mobility. There are also social reasons why elderly people may not eat well:

- if they live alone they may not feel like cooking for one
- they may not be able to afford the food they would like to eat
- they may find it hard to get out to the shops
- they may find it physically difficult to cook, but pre-prepared meals may be too large for them
- they may get little or no pleasure from eating because of uncomfortable false teeth or diminished sense of smell and taste.

It can be difficult to motivate yourself to cook if you live alone

FIND IT OUT

THE JARGON DRAGON

nutritionally deficient –
lacking in the correct levels
of vitamins and minerals for a
healthy body

People with a disability

People with a disability are no more likely to be **nutritionally deficient** than any other group. It depends on the nature of the disability and the individual concerned. Where mobility is restricted, weight gain may be a problem, in which case a reduced calorie intake may be necessary. If you need to plan or cook meals for children or people with disabilities, then you will need to check their dietary requirements with them or with their carers.

> *Why do you think a person who uses a wheelchair may be likely to gain weight?*

Regular exercise

Exercise has many benefits

Exercise is fun! You will also feel better for it. But even if you have exercised regularly, it is easy to lose the habit if you give it up for a short time.

Exercise improves your stamina, suppleness and strength, but the benefits will depend on how vigorously and regularly the activity is carried out. If you exercise vigorously but not very often, you are shocking your body into action and your muscles are jolted into performance. On the other hand, if you exercise gradually at first and then build up regularly, your body becomes accustomed to the increased pressure. Your limbs become more flexible and your heart and lungs increase their capacity to supply the body with its extra demands for oxygen.

People are less likely to maintain an exercise plan if it is not suited to their lifestyle. It is far better to set realistic targets that they can fit into their routine and that they can manage. It is also better for their self-esteem to succeed in keeping to a regular exercise pattern than to start enthusiastically and then trail off.

Exercise can be part of your social life

Supportive relationships

Some relationships are very important to us, namely those with family and close friends. When we are with our close friends or family we feel we can be ourselves. We often do and say things that we wouldn't in an 'outside' or formal setting with people we do not know very well. In an ideal relationship with family and close friends, we can say we are sure of care and unconditional love. These close relationships are called informal supportive relationships.

A different type of relationship exists between such people as students and teachers, bosses and staff, or doctors and patients. In these relationships, there is a less relaxed way of speaking and behaving than with close friends or family. These relationships are called formal supportive relationships.

To get on well in society, we need to have both types of relationship.

FIND IT OUT

Fill in the spaces in the table below. The first two have been completed for you to give you a start:

Informal supportive relationships	Formal supportive relationships
Parent	Teacher
Best friend	Doctor

Positive formal relationships such as those between teacher and students, are another important aspect of a person's well-being

Adequate finance resources

People need enough money to maintain a positive healthy lifestyle. Poverty and ill-health go together. Surveys show that families on an adequate income suffer fewer episodes of ill-health than families on low income.

A government report in 1980, called The Black Report, highlighted inequalities according to the social class of people. This report found that people on low income are more likely to become ill with certain diseases. These increased rates of disease occur over the whole of a person's life. It also appears that these differences between people on high and low income are on the increase.

People who have an adequate income are more likely to have access to proper medical care and to use health promotion information. They are also less likely to suffer from nutritional problems because they can buy nutritious food.

People living in lower income areas may also suffer these negative effects upon their health and well-being:

- there may be fewer schools or schools that are not very good near by
- there may not be many medical facilities in the locality
- the housing may be poorer
- there may be environmental pollution (if they live near factories or busy roads for example).

Poorer housing can have an adverse effect on health and well-being

What is meant by the term 'health postcode lottery'?

FIND
IT
OUT

Stimulating work, education and leisure activity

Taking part in stimulating work, education and leisure activities can reduce stress, and also improve your physical health and well-being. Such activities include physical pursuits such as playing sport and walking and less physical activities such as watching sport, TV, meeting friends, reading and listening to music. Leisure or recreational activities can mean different things to different people, depending on their situation and interests. Some people might enjoy reading, while others may like walking or do-it-yourself. Leisure activities of all sorts contribute to health and well-being and to the overall quality of people's lives.

Surveys show that indoor leisure pursuits are more popular than outdoor ones in the UK. Watching TV seems to be the most popular activity, while going out for a drink is an activity that over half of adults take part in.

Different factors influence people's ability to take part in recreational activities. For example, in some cultures it may be considered unsuitable for women to take part in certain sports such as swimming. Participation may also be restricted because of cost, lack of time or access difficulties. People on low income may not be able to afford the entrance fees and people with disabilities may not be able to take part because of inadequate physical access.

Recreational activities can be classified as those involving:

- **physical** exercise
- meeting other people in a **social** setting
- **emotional** and **intellectual** activity.

Some activities may fall into more than one of these groups. For example, dancing is a physical activity in a social setting, while a pub quiz night is an intellectual activity in a social setting.

The activities are all linked because they involve the development and maintenance of physical, social, emotional and intellectual well-being.

Physical benefits
Physical activity contributes to fitness and well-being in several ways:

- Strength – the ability of muscles to work over short periods of time. It is required for lifting or in the act of jumping.
- Stamina – the ability of muscles to continue working without fatigue (becoming tired).
- Suppleness – the flexibility of the joints. Exercise to develop suppleness is part of warming up and avoids strains to muscles and joints.

- Speed of reaction – the ability to respond rapidly to changes. This is linked to hand-eye co-ordination, improved balance and agility.
- Heart and **lung efficiency** – regular physical recreation makes the heart, lungs and circulation work to provide oxygen to the body effectively. This reduces the risk of heart disease.
- Determination – regular physical activity also develops a determination to follow tasks through to a finish.

lung efficiency – how well the lungs work

Intellectual benefits

You may think that all your mental activity should be confined to school, college or work, and that recreation should be relaxing. Intellectual activity can, however, provide a stimulating, satisfying and, at the same time, relaxing recreation. These types of activity often involve problem-solving in some way. This may be in terms of strategies in games such as chess.

List at least five leisure activities that involve some form of problem-solving.

FIND IT OUT

Intellectual activity can be a part of socialising as well

Reading also provides an intellectual stimulus. Reading for relaxation can involve stories that stimulate your imagination. Using your imagination stimulates mental activity and satisfaction in the enjoyment of the story. Many books also involve problem-solving as part of the enjoyment; for example mysteries and detective stories often give sufficient information to enable you to solve the problem before the main characters.

Many hobbies that involve collecting, learning new skills (such as playing musical instruments) or making objects (models or pottery) involve intellectual skills. Meeting with others to pursue these hobbies in clubs and societies also provides some of the social benefits of recreation.

Benefits of recreation for different people

From what you have already read in this section, you will have the tools to think about the aspects of recreational activities that affect choice. For activities to be beneficial they need to match the needs and abilities of the individuals. There should also be a balance in terms of physical, social and intellectual pursuits.

Children – The major recreational activity for children is play. Play provides physical, intellectual and social benefits. The type of play will depend upon the stage of development of the child. Some physical activities, such as swimming (with the proper aids), are appropriate for children of all ages. Other activities such as team games (football, hockey, netball, etc.) require physical, intellectual and social development before they are suitable. Young children may not have:

- the physical co-ordination to catch or hit a ball
- the intellectual development to understand rules
- the social development to play co-operatively in a team.

Much recreation for young children occurs in and around the home. Often it involves supervision and co-operation from an adult. Typical activities and their benefits include:

- drawing, painting and colouring – physical and intellectual
- looking at books – intellectual
- playing with dolls – social, emotional and intellectual
- dressing up – intellectual, emotional and social
- pretend cooking – intellectual, emotional, social and physical.

Board games can provide intellectual stimulation for children

As children get older the availability of organised recreational activities increases. The child's development makes organised team games possible. Parental involvement may decrease and the child may undertake some recreation in places like playgrounds and parks, away from home and parental supervision.

Adolescents – Once children become adolescents, their independence increases. There may be easier access to recreation outside the home. The range of activities includes social gatherings in youth clubs and other organised functions.

For many people adolescence is a time of peak physical fitness. It is also a time when recreation patterns become established and are maintained throughout the rest of life. Access to and availability of recreation facilities can be very important.

The social aspect of recreational activities is very important during adolescence. It is a time when relationships are being explored and many recreational activities involve social groupings.

Why are social peer groups so important to teenagers?

FIND IT OUT

Older people – A common stereotype of older people states that physical recreation, education or work has to be limited. This view is incorrect. The important thing is to make sure that the physical recreation is appropriate. Care needs to be taken to ensure that the activities help maintain the body, rather than damage it. Remember that:

- older people are not at a peak of physical fitness
- reaction speeds reduce with age
- bones become more fragile and injuries take longer to heal
- heart, lungs and circulation are less efficient than when they were much younger.

All of these factors will affect the choice of activity. Often re-creation that is physical and also has a social focus is appropriate.

Many older people play bowls. In fact, it is even a bit of a cliché! However, it meets their needs on many counts. It involves some physical activity. There is a very strong social element of meeting with other people and having time to talk. The skill of controlling the ball and playing to win involves an intellectual challenge.

People with physical disabilities – Physical disabilities cover a very wide range, including:

- visual impairment
- hearing impairment
- wheelchair users
- those with a limited range of movements (such as severe arthritis)
- those with poor muscle control (such as cerebral palsy, Parkinson's disease, multiple sclerosis).

Find out the effects on the body of arthritis, cerebral palsy, Parkinson's disease and multiple sclerosis.

While some people with disabilities may feel unable to participate in some recreational activities, most will be able to identify activities they would like to undertake. In many cases, the recreational activity can be adapted to support the specific need of the person.

People with disabilities have the same needs for recreation as everyone else, namely physical recreation, intellectual recreation and education. Physical activities may also have an important health-related role in improving mobility.

Jim

case study

Jim is 70. He is a very heavy smoker. He is a retired teacher who lives alone in a small cottage on the outskirts of a large town. Jim is 1.8 m tall (5ft 10in) and weighs 84kg (13 stone). He likes to think of himself as fit, but when he has to run for the bus he becomes breathless.

Jim cooks for himself, but he tends to eat food such as cheese, steak, chips, burgers and eggs. His eating habits are irregular. Some days he will cook three meals; some days he eats just one and has only coffee for breakfast.

He drinks two cans of lager and a glass of whisky every night as he watches television alone, he has few friends and the cottages on both sides of his are holiday lets, so are empty in the winter.

Q *What are the main features of Jim's lifestyle?*

Describe Jim's diet. What could he do to improve it?

Check Jim's weight and height against the weight/ height chart on page 123. What advice would you give him about his weight?

How could Jim increase the amount of exercise he takes?

What are the dangers to Jim's health of smoking and regular alcohol drinking?

People with disabilities have the same needs for recreation as everyone else

Activities are often organised for people with similar disabilities, but these have their limitations. They can be very useful as self-help groups, but they do tend to limit contact with others. The reactions of able-bodied people to those with disabilities provide a barrier to many activities in general. This can cause feelings of isolation from society, with social links only developing among other people with similar disabilities.

Use of health monitoring and illness prevention services

Many diseases are preventable, but prevention depends on achieving high levels within the population of vaccination, screening and monitoring.

One of the most common causes of death among children aged 1–14 is as a result of infections. This does not seem to vary between social classes. The government has set up health monitoring and immunisation programmes to try and reduce the numbers of these deaths.

FIND IT OUT

Find out what you can about the classification of people into 'social classes'.

Vaccination

Health Authorities and the government set targets for immunisation with the aim that about 95 per cent of children are vaccinated for diphtheria, polio, tetanus and MMR (measles, mumps and rubella). Girls are also vaccinated against rubella at about the age of 10 to protect their unborn children if they become pregnant later in life.

Politicians refer to 'herd immunity', which means that if most people are immune to a disease, this will reduce the chances of it spreading. There is disagreement, however, both over the percentages, and over the basic ideas of herd immunity.

Vaccination (or immunisation) programmes are usually carried out by general practitioners. Health visitors also have a responsibility for monitoring immunisation, identifying children to be vaccinated.

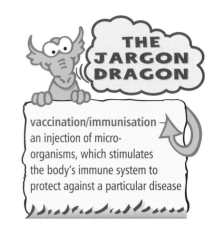

THE JARGON DRAGON

vaccination/immunisation – an injection of micro-organisms, which stimulates the body's immune system to protect against a particular disease

A new guide to
childhood immunisations
for babies up to 15 months

Prevention of disease depends on encouraging most people to immunise their children

Screening

The government has asked Health Authorities to set up screening systems for cervical and breast cancers. This means that all the relevant people in an age group are called for a check-up at regular intervals.

The cervical cancer programme consists of:

- a computerised system to call and re-call women for screening
- an invitation to all women between 20 and 64 for screening
- a re-call every five years.

Despite the setting up of these systems many women still ignore their appointments. This may be because they are afraid, lack adequate information or don't like the impersonal computer-issued invitations.

The breast cancer screening programme aims to ensure that all women between the ages of 50 and 64 are called for screening every three years. There are doubts, however, as to whether screening significantly reduces the number of deaths from this disease. Some people in the care professions also argue that the screening programme may possibly do more harm than good by causing unnecessary mastectomies and emotional distress.

What is breast screening?

- Breast screening (mammography) is an x-ray examination of the breasts.
- Breast screening can show breast cancers at an early stage, when they are too small for you or your doctor to see or feel.
- A mammogram takes a few minutes and involves a tiny dose of radiation, so the risk to your health is very small.
- Your whole visit to the breast screening unit should take about half an hour.

Why do I need breast screening?

One in nine women will develop breast cancer at some time in their life. Breast cancer is more common in women over 50. Breast screening can help to find small changes in the breast before there are any other signs or symptoms. If changes are found at an early stage, there is a good chance of a successful recovery.

Should all women have breast screening?

We invite all women aged between 50 and 64 for breast screening every three years.

Breast screening for women under 50 has not been proven to reduce the number of deaths from breast cancer. However, whatever age you are, if you are ever worried about any breast problem, please contact your doctor who may refer you for a specialist opinion if necessary.

We are gradually changing the automatic invitation system to include women up to 70 years old. At the moment, if you are 65 or over, you will not automatically be invited for screening but you will be screened for free every three years if you ask for it.

Please contact your local breast screening office or your doctor for advice.

2

3

This breast screening leaflet provides information to encourage women to take part in the programme

Risk management

Weighing up the possibility of injury or accident as against the benefits of an activity is called risk management (see risks to health and safety on page 95).

General advice is to work up gradually to a high level of physical activity. This enables the body to develop the strength necessary and also encourages weight loss. For this purpose, there are many groups that offer recreation (associated with weight loss) for **obese** people. For many of these, there is a financial cost that needs to be considered.

THE JARGON DRAGON

obese – very overweight to the extent of risking health

Health and safety is also a consideration for people with heart and **circulatory problems**. Physical recreation for them needs to be supervised and monitored.

There are two risk issues involved in developing a health improvement plan for people who are obese and those who have heart and circulatory problems. These are related to self-esteem and health and safety.

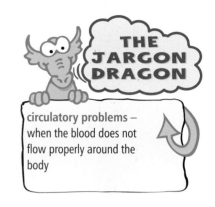

circulatory problems – when the blood does not flow properly around the body

Risks to self-esteem

Any recreational activity that exposes a person to embarrassment will lower his or her self-esteem. An obese person may feel unable to participate in an activity because of worry about the possible comments of others. Self-help groups can be useful here.

In health terms, an obese person needs to lose weight. Recreation may be directed to this, with physical activity and diet contributing. If the physical activity is carried out with others who are obese, the embarrassment factor can be reduced. There is also an element of understanding and pressure from others in the same boat, which helps a person to continue in the activity. The social aspect of this kind of recreation is important.

Why is it important for a person's self-esteem that a risk management assessment be carried out before they undertake any health improvement plan?

Risks to health and safety

An obese person should undertake physical activity under guidance from a health practitioner. The strain of exercise on joints, muscles and the heart needs to be monitored carefully. People with heart and circulatory disorders must also be guided by their health practitioner before undertaking physical activity.

Swimming is a very appropriate activity for both obese people and those with heart and circulatory disorders. The buoyancy provided by the water reduces the stresses on joints and the exercise can be tailored to meet needs. Swimming provides exercise that improves muscle tone and joint flexibility. It improves breathing and increases the heart rate, which both benefit the respiratory and circulatory systems.

Providers of recreation facilities need to be concerned about health and safety

Risks to health and well-being

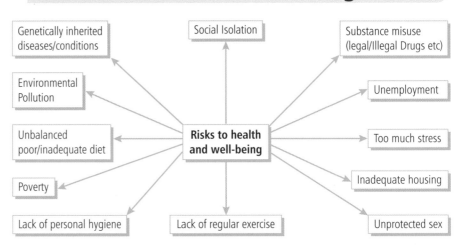

Genetically inherited diseases/conditions

Social Isolation

Substance misuse (legal/Illegal Drugs etc)

Environmental Pollution

Unemployment

Unbalanced poor/inadequate diet

Risks to health and well-being

Too much stress

Poverty

Inadequate housing

Lack of personal hygiene

Lack of regular exercise

Unprotected sex

This section will help you understand about the many factors that can put people's health and well-being at risk. It will help you to identify the lifestyle factors over which people have control, and also the genetic, social and economic factors that individuals may not be able to change.

Genetically inherited diseases and conditions

At <u>conception</u> every person is provided with a mix of genetic material from his or her parents. This genetic make-up governs much of the person's later development. Many disorders of later life are as a result of these inherited <u>genes</u>.

Gene disorders – A person inherits two copies of most genes: one from the mother and one from the father. If two 'abnormal' genes are inherited, then the function of the 'normal' gene is lost. The 'normal' gene can mask the 'abnormal' gene and so people can carry the defective gene and pass it on without showing any effects themselves. In this way some disorders, called recessive disorders, can skip generations in families.

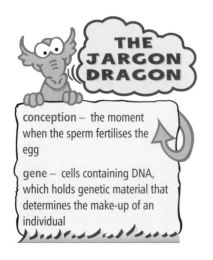

THE JARGON DRAGON

conception – the moment when the sperm fertilises the egg

gene – cells containing DNA, which holds genetic material that determines the make-up of an individual

With some disorders, the presence of the 'abnormal' gene always has an effect. If the gene is sufficiently dominant (or powerful), just one copy brings about the full 'abnormality'.

Inherited gene disorders – Just as we inherit characteristics such as eye colour from our parents, and a tendency to conditions such as asthma and heart disease, so we can also inherit defective genes from our parents that give rise to ill-health. Included in this category are disorders of a single gene, such as:

- cystic fibrosis
- Huntington's chorea
- sickle cell anaemia
- colour blindness.

Find out what are the symptoms of cystic fibrosis, Huntington's chorea, sickle cell anaemia and colour blindness.

People with learning disabilities can nevertheless enter the job market

Substance abuse

Cigarettes, alcohol and illegal drugs are used to change feelings and moods. They can cause a lowering of stress levels and enhance feelings of well-being. They are all, to a greater or lesser extent, addictive and can all cause harm both to the user and others if they are misused. The use of alcohol and cigarettes is legal and more socially acceptable than the use of drugs. However, there is increasing opposition to smoking in public places and many people regard smoking as anti-social behaviour.

Smoking – Most smokers wish that they had never started to smoke, not least because of the health risks that they face. Many young people smoke and most of those who smoke become dependent on cigarettes and have difficulty in giving them up, even though nearly everyone knows that smoking causes cancer.

The well-documented risks to health and well-being of smoking are worth repeating here:

- Lung cancer – nearly 90 per cent of cases of lung cancer are caused by smoking and a large percentage of people with lung cancer are dead within two years of diagnosis. Smokers are four times more at risk from lung cancer than non-smokers even if they do not inhale.
- Bronchitis – this is a serious inflammation of the tubes leading to the lungs. Bronchitis can also affect non-smokers, but it is more common and worse in smokers.
- Emphysema – this is caused by the destruction of the feathery branches that transport oxygen deep in the lungs. People suffering from the condition are initially short of breath, but eventually become so dependent on oxygen supplies that they can hardly move outside their own home. Nine out of ten cases of emphysema are caused by smoking.
- Hardening of the arteries – the 'furring up' of the arteries of the heart is another condition associated with smoking. This makes it extremely painful to move around and can lead to amputation of limbs. A heart attack occurs when one of the arteries becomes completely blocked by a blood clot and this can kill.
- Heart disease – smoking contributes to a quarter of deaths from heart disease. Nicotine in cigarettes may be involved here, because it makes the heart beat faster so the heart's requirement for oxygen is greater.
- Cervical cancer – women who smoke run twice the risk of cancer of the cervix than women who do not smoke.
- Miscarriage – pregnant women, even those smoking fewer than 20 cigarettes per day, are 20 per cent more likely to miscarry. Premature births and stillbirths are also more common among smokers than non-smokers. The same is true for **infertility.**
- Gum disease – smokers are more likely to have gum disease and consequently problems with their teeth.

THE JARGON DRAGON

infertility – inability to conceive and deliver a baby

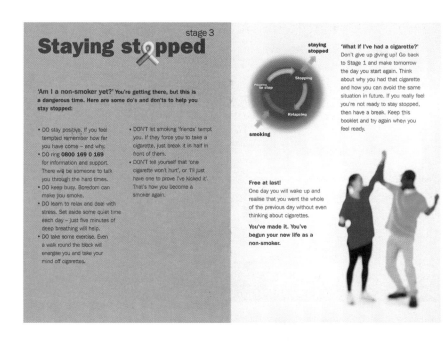

Anti-smoking leaflets encourage smokers to give up

Passive smoking – The health risks from smoking are undoubtedly heavy. However, other people who may not smoke themselves also run the risks of ill-health if they live or work in a smoky atmosphere. Such people are termed passive smokers. They are vulnerable to the same diseases, as listed above, but to a lesser extent.

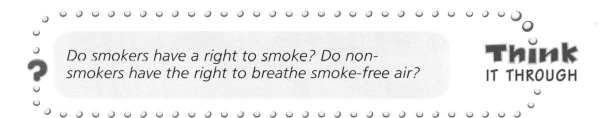

? *Do smokers have a right to smoke? Do non-smokers have the right to breathe smoke-free air?*

Think
IT THROUGH

It is very difficult to estimate the risk of passive smoking, but two studies of children with parents who both smoked estimated that the children breathed in the equivalent amount of smoke as that associated with actively smoking 80 to 150 cigarettes per year.

Passive smoking can also aggravate asthma and other conditions affecting the lungs.

Group pressure often leads people to become addicted to drugs like tobacco

FIND IT OUT

Conduct a small survey on smoking among people you know. Ask some friends and members of your family the following questions:

- *Do you smoke?*
- *Why do you (or do you not) smoke?*
- *Do you know of any dangers from smoking?*

Present the results of your survey to the class.

Alcohol abuse – Unlike smoking, drinking alcohol is still socially acceptable. The majority of adults drink alcohol and consumption has doubled since the 1950s. To refuse alcohol may seem embarrassing. You may think that people will consider you odd or cranky if you refuse a drink. Do not forget that alcohol is in fact a drug. It is a legal, socially accepted drug, but one that can cause much personal and social damage.

Alcohol is formed by the fermentation action of yeasts on various fruits or cereals. The resulting liquid, with various additions, may be drunk as wines or beers. Distilling or boiling off to produce spirits, such as whisky, gin or vodka, may further concentrate the alcohol. Different drinks contain different amounts of alcohol.

'HOW MUCH DO I DRINK?'

If you want to work out how much you drink, you need to ask yourself three questions:

● how much do I usually drink on a weekday?

● how much do I usually drink on a Friday night, Saturday and Sunday?

● how much do I drink on a special occasion, like having friends over, someone's birthday or a wedding?

You may find it helps to fill out the drinks diary on pages 8 and 9. Don't forget to include any drinks you have with a meal, and 'extras' like a can or two when you're watching sport on the telly, or a glass of wine while you're cooking, or a tot of something in a hot drink. It all adds up.

Having recorded how much you're drinking, you need to work out how much pure alcohol (ethanol) you're consuming.

Advice on how much alcohol is reasonable

When the police stop drivers suspected of 'driving while under the influence of drink', they measure the blood alcohol concentration – BAC. This is the concentration of alcohol in the body's system. The legal limit for driving is 80mg per 100ml BAC, so an averaged-sized man would be around the legal limit for driving if he has drunk five units or 2.5 pints of ordinary beer (or its equivalent). A smaller man or a woman may be *above* the BAC legal limit after drinking five units of alcohol.

Any alcohol, even a small drink, will **impair driving ability**

Alcohol takes effect quickly but wears off slowly.

The only safe course is not to drink and drive.

Alcohol is quickly absorbed into the bloodstream, affecting the brain and impairing driving ability.

After drinking a half pint of ordinary strength beer

10 MINUTES
After just 10 minutes, 50% of the alcohol consumed will have been absorbed into the bloodstream.

60 MINUTES
After an hour all the alcohol will have been absorbed.

Absorption is accelerated still further when drinking on an empty stomach. Long drinks made with mixers have a faster effect as they enter the bloodstream quicker.

Getting rid of alcohol

MIDNIGHT
At midnight, after an evening's drinking there may be 200mg/100ml of alcohol in the blood.

7.30am
On getting up, there is still 90mg/100ml. You are still over the current legal limit and unfit to drive.

MIDDAY
By lunchtime, elimination has continued to around 20mg/100ml. Your driving may still be impaired.

It is impossible to speed up alcohol elimination. Neither a shower, nor a cup of coffee, nor other ways of "sobering up" will help. It just takes time.

Getting rid of alcohol is a much slower process requiring hours rather than minutes.

"How to make sure it isn't you": part of a leaflet prodced by the Department of the Environment, Transport and the Regions (DETR)

The factors affecting alcohol concentration in the body are:

- the amount of alcohol consumed
- the size of the drinker
- the sex of the drinker (women have proportionately less body fluid than men and are therefore less able to absorb alcohol)
- the rate at which drinks are consumed
- the amount of food in the stomach.

Drug abuse – Drug abuse means those forms of drug taking that meet with social disapproval. This includes possession, for non-medical use, of illegal drugs under the Misuse of Drugs Act 1972. Cannabis, LSD, opiates, amphetamines and solvents are all illegal drugs.

There are many leaflets giving information on the dangers of drugs and how people can get help

People take illegal drugs for all sorts of reasons, ranging from curiosity to searching for some form of escape. Studies indicate four main reasons why people take drugs:

- a mixture of curiosity and pleasure seeking
- encouragement from peers
- to relieve stress or solve problems, but mostly as a gesture of rebellion rather than deep anxiety
- availability – if drugs are around at a party or concert there is often pressure to take them.

Solvents – A large number of solvents can be abused by sniffing the vapours or gases released, from glue, paint and petrol to lighter fuel. The vapours act as a depressant and hallucinations can be experienced when solvents are inhaled.

"Your questions answered": information about solvent abuse

Solvents
(Lighter Fluid & Gas, Correction Fluid, Thinners, Aerosols, Petrol, Glue)

What is it?
When the vapours are inhaled, some substances produce an effect similar to alcohol. Some are used as solvents, while others are propellant gases. The greatest danger with solvent abuse is that death can occur the first time a person "sniffs".

What are the short term effects?
The effects are similar to being drunk. Users feel dizzy, giggly and light-headed. There is a risk of hallucinations. Accidents are likely to occur because of impaired judgement. Spraying directly into the throat greatly increases the dangers. Users can be left with a "hangover" effect after sniffing.

What are the long term effects?
Tolerance develops and, in some cases, psychological dependence can occur. Heavy regular use can lead to brain, liver and kidney damage.

What does the Law say?
It is illegal for shopkeepers to sell to under 18's if they believe the product is going to be abused.

21

Accidental death or injury can happen after solvent abuse when the 'sniffer' (solvent user) loses control, especially if they are sniffing in an unsafe environment, such as on a roof or near a canal. Sniffing to the point of becoming unconscious risks death through choking on vomit. Very long-term use might cause brain damage. The after-effects of poor concentration, fatigue and forgetfulness can become habitual and affect whole lifestyles and opportunities.

It is an offence for shopkeepers to sell potentially dangerous solvents to people under 18 years of age.

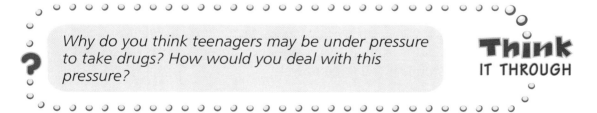

Why do you think teenagers may be under pressure to take drugs? How would you deal with this pressure?

Think IT THROUGH

Everyday legal 'drugs' and their effect upon health and well-being – The drugs discussed above are illegal and potentially very dangerous. It is interesting to note, however, that tea, coffee and cocoa all contain active chemicals such as caffeine, which are absorbed into the bloodstream.

The structure of these chemicals is similar to that of adrenalin, the body's own stimulant.

People who drink more than two cups of coffee or four cups of tea per day will have levels of chemicals in their bloodstream that will keep their 'rate of arousal' at a higher than normal level. Maintaining an artificially high level of arousal will reduce your ability to cope with any additional stress, and will keep your body and mind in perpetual tension. When tea and coffee intake is reduced you may well feel lethargic and slow for a few days. You may even develop a 'coffee withdrawal' headache. The table below shows a list of caffeine indicators.

Amounts of caffeine in different food and drink

Food or drink	Amount of caffeine
1 cup of instant coffee	90mg
1 cup of filter coffee	200mg
1 cup of tea (depending on how long you allow it to brew)	40–70mg
1 can of cola	40mg
1 150g bar of plain chocolate	100mg
1 150g bar of milk chocolate	30mg

An unbalanced, poor quality or inadequate diet

Diet and health – The influence of diet on health has long been recognised. A healthy diet promotes energy and growth and provides the basis for a healthy life. If we want to feel well, stay fit, have good teeth and keep our weight in proportion to our size, then we need to think about the foods we eat. It is possible to eat nothing but biscuits, chocolates, crisps and cakes for a day or two without feeling too many ill-effects, but if we continued with this type of diet for longer we would begin to put on weight, be at greater risk from holes in our teeth and generally feel less fit. Dietary factors play a significant part in deaths from heart disease and cancers such as cancer of the stomach and large bowel.

The current recommendations for a healthy diet include:

- eating more fibre
- eating less sugar
- eating less fat.

All of these recommendations could be implemented by simple changes in the daily diet.

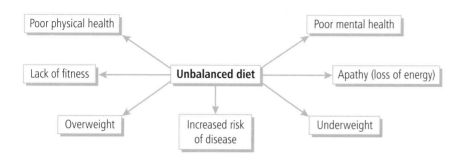

The harmful effects of an unbalanced diet

Your diet is unbalanced when you are eating the wrong types and amount of food for the energy you are using.

Too many fats and carbohydrates and too little exercise can make you too fat or obese. At the same time, you can become ill if you don't eat enough foods that contain the necessary minerals and vitamins. You may become malnourished or suffer from malnutrition (*mal* means bad). The key word to remember is 'balanced'.

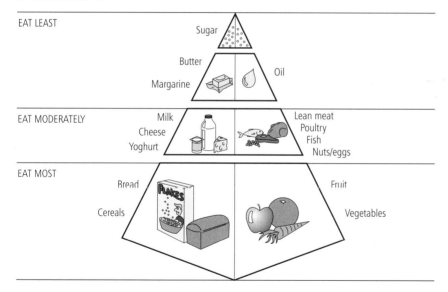

The nutrient triangle

A balanced diet must take into account a person's size, sex, age, state of well-being (how healthy they are), how much exercise they take, food intake and the environment (how hot or cold it is).

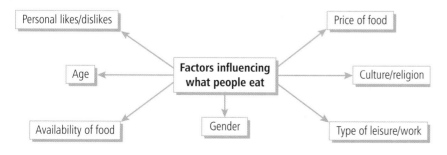

"Get Healthy" and "The Guide to Grazing", just two of the many leaflets that encourage good eating habits

The body is able to adapt to reduced food intake, but too little food over a period of time can lead to ill-health through under-nutrition. In extreme cases, as in developing countries of the world, starvation causes stunting of physical and mental development and wasting (this means *becoming weak*). Diseases like scurvy and some forms of anaemia are caused by a deficiency (shortage) of certain nutrients or by the body's inability to absorb those nutrients.

In the UK, starvation may be less of a problem, but excessive amounts of food can also cause malnutrition which may in turn lead to conditions of ill-health such as obesity, heart disease or high blood pressure.

Water – Water is not usually regarded as a food, but it is vital in the diet. Every part and function of the body depends on water and it is being lost continuously through the skin, lungs, kidneys and bowels. This water must be replaced and is obtained from the liquids that we drink and the food that we eat.

Too much stress

Most people are aware that too much stress can endanger your health, but too little stress can also be bad for you. People who have few demands made on them or who have little stimulation may find themselves feeling very tired without doing very much or wanting to do very much. Some people thrive on stress, but others find even a minimal amount difficult to cope with.

A definition of stress – Stress is a response. It is the imbalance between an individual and the demands made of that individual. An extreme and sudden stress produces a physical reaction. For example, if you think a child is about to run out in front of a car, your body may go through the following series of reactions:

- Your eyes and ears receive an alarm signal.
- Your brain registers that the child is in danger and sends messages out along the nerves.
- Your muscles contract in readiness for action.
- The strength of your heartbeat increases so blood is pumped more quickly to where it is most needed, i.e. your muscles.
- Chemicals in the brain set off a number of hormonal changes in your body.
- Adrenalin is produced.
- Your hearing becomes more sensitive.
- Your skin goes pale because the blood has to go elsewhere.
- Your breathing gets faster.
- Your blood pressure rises, carrying oxygen more quickly to the heart, muscles and brain.
- Your sweating increases.
- You may be left feeling faint because the fear causes you to breathe too fast, leading to less blood in the brain.

Reactions to stress – People may react differently to stress or have different reactions at different times. There are three types of reaction. For example, if you are engrossed in a piece of homework and some friends call round, you might take a:

- fight response – you throw down your pen, open the door muttering irritably that you are busy

- flight response – you think to yourself that you might as well take a break and put the kettle on

- flow response – neither fighting nor running away, but going with the flow: your entertain your friends for a while, then send them away and finish your work.

No one response is better than another. Overuse of one particular response, however, may lead to a fixed, rigid pattern and eventually to a stressed state.

Obviously, the responses outlined here are broad stereotypes, and many people fall between these categories, or may vary from one type to another.

Causes of stress – Stress is a highly individual matter. Different things cause stress in different people. Noisy or hazardous environments, difficult relationships or work may all be stressful. Experts acknowledge that major life changes, such as going to school for the first time, getting married, having a baby, buying a house, getting divorced and bereavement are generally stressful.

Below are listed some of the factors people find stressful about work, which may be very difficult to cope with:

- Money worries. Your income is low. You cannot earn more. Your job is not secure.
- Relationship problems. You do not get on well with some or all of your colleagues. You are forced to work with people you do not like.
- Enduring poor working conditions. You have to put up with noise, vibration, poor lighting, heat, cold, poor ventilation, danger from physical or chemical hazards, fear of accidents, dirt and grime, long hours of overtime and shift work.
- Problems with work load. You have too much or not enough responsibility or work to handle.
- Lack of prospects. There is no hope of promotion or advancement.
- Lack of recognition. No one appreciates what you do.
- Low satisfaction. The job is boring and you have too much time on your hands or it is so demanding you have no time left for yourself.
- Shifting goals. You do not feel you can ever achieve or finish anything because the demands are constantly changing.

Lack of personal hygiene

Personal hygiene is important and is a way of maintaining good health. Use of soap and hot water in washing removes bacteria from the skin. It also removes dead skin cells and oils that provide a food source for bacteria and fungi.

Poor personal hygiene causes the spread of diseases more than anything else. The common cold and influenza (flu) are spread by droplets coughed or sneezed out by an infected person. They

Find out what the words 'bacteria' and 'fungi' mean in relation to personal hygiene.

are also breathed out, but do not spread as far. Failure to use handkerchiefs (preferably disposable tissues) increases the spread.

Hygiene issues are important for everyone, but especially for the following groups of people:

- Young babies are less resistant to disease and may suffer more damage from even mild doses of food poisoning. Hygiene levels need to be higher than for healthy adults.
- Older people are also vulnerable to mild doses of food poisoning.
- For older people who are reliant on others for care, issues of personal hygiene are important. Ensuring that they are clean is not sufficient. Carers must look after other aspects of grooming such as hair and nail care. Shaving or trimming facial hair is important for men (even beards and moustaches need trimming). By paying attention to personal hygiene for these people, and supporting its achievement, you not only maintain physical health but you also promote emotional well-being.

Feet – Toe-nails should be kept short and hard skin removed, but anything more major like athlete's foot, bunions or corns should be seen by a doctor or a **chiropodist**. It may be tempting to squeeze feet into fashionable shoes but this can cause deformities later. Children's feet are particularly vulnerable in this way and it is best to have their feet measured and shoes properly fitted.

The need for professional care for feet increases with age. Some elderly people may need to see a chiropodist regularly.

Unprotected sex

Some infections can be passed on as a result of unsafe sexual behaviour. This is sometimes known as sexual infection or sexually transmitted disease (STD).

People may feel embarrassed if they have a sexually transmitted infection, but in fact, apart from the common cold, STDs are the most common type of infection.

The main STDs are syphilis, gonorrhoea, thrush, genital herpes, genital warts and hepatitis.

Avoiding STDs – Sexual activity is most appropriate within a secure, loving relationship where partners have respect for each other. The following checklist explains how to prevent STDs:

- Don't take risks.
- Know and understand about 'safe sex'. Use condoms.
- Remember that STDs are no respecters of anyone – everyone is at risk.
- Restrict the number of sexual partners.
- Practise good personal hygiene.

AIDS – AIDS stands for Acquired Immune Deficiency Syndrome:

- Acquired – it is caught from someone or something.
- Immune deficiency – you have an immune deficiency when your body cannot defend itself against certain illnesses.
- Syndrome – the particular pattern of illnesses you can get as a result. AIDS is a disease, which results from contracting HIV (Human Immune Deficiency Virus).

The main groups at risk from AIDS are:

- sexual partners of AIDS sufferers or virus carriers
- male homosexuals and bisexuals
- drug addicts
- sufferers of a blood clotting disorder called haemophilia
- babies born to AIDS sufferers or virus carriers
- prostitutes (both male and female).

However, all sexually active people are at risk if they have several partners and do not protect themselves (see list above in the section on STDs).

People who contract AIDS may be ill for nine months to six years. About half die within a year of diagnosis. Once a diagnosis of AIDS is made it obviously has many far-reaching implications, practically, socially and medically, for the individual. There is no cure at present for the disease.

Help is available from GU (genito–urinary) clinics, which can give general advice about AIDS. They can give the HIV antibody test (the test, also available from GPs, that shows if a person is HIV positive and so has the virus that could develop into AIDS), and offer special advice and counselling from people who have the virus or AIDS itself. The advice and treatment is free and confidential. People do not need a letter from their doctor. GU clinics can also give detailed information on what is 'safe sex' and what is 'risky sex'.

Social isolation

People are not naturally social animals; they have to learn how to be sociable. To be social animals we need to know how to interact with other people.

The need for social contact is recognised in most caring systems. For older people, there is a risk of isolation. Where a husband or wife dies the surviving partner may be left alone with little contact with other people. This isolation can be worsened by difficulties in moving out of the house. Many Social Services Departments recognise this and organise day centres to support people by coming together for social contact. Other recreational activities are often provided to support this. Dances, bingo and special swimming sessions for older people, for example, all help maintain social interaction.

Many Social Services Departments recognise that the need for social contact is as important as the physical care

Any social interaction helps people to understand each other. For adolescents, the social interaction may be in situations where individuals can start to explore relationships. Many youth clubs, discos and youth organisations are offered to provide an opportunity for individuals to meet and learn about each other, and in some cases develop relationships.

Shared recreational activities imply shared interests. This is the first step towards friendship. The benefits of recreational activities are normally a mixture of physical, intellectual and social. The mixture contributes to a balanced personality and a balanced lifestyle.

In all of these cases, the choice of recreation has to be made to provide for the need of the individual. To suggest that a person living alone undertakes solitary recreation, such as jogging, does not meet the need for social recreation. To encourage an obese person to take up physical activities involving strenuous exercise could be dangerous to that person's health. An obese person may also be embarrassed to exercise in public.

Poverty

Many of the inequalities in health care caused by poverty were highlighted by The Black Report, published in 1980, but still relevant today. This government report provided evidence of a distinct social class structure in health provision. In other words, people with a higher income get better health care than people with a lower income.

The Black Report revealed that people with a higher income receive more preventive health treatment than do people with a lower income. People with a higher income are also treated by more experienced doctors, and do not have to wait as long to be seen.

Poverty and unemployment are major causes of ill-health. The consequences of unemployment include stress, bad diet and inadequate housing. Examples of illnesses that increase with the unemployment figures are alcoholism, heart disease, psychiatric illness, indigestion, arthritis and high blood pressure.

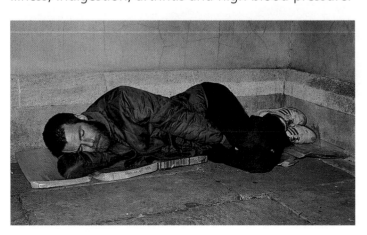

Homelessness can have a devastating effect on a person's health and well-being

> *What is psychiatric illness?*

Inadequate housing

For many people, home is not only a place of accommodation, but also a source of their physical and mental well-being. Home should be a place where you can relax, away from the tensions and pressures of work or school. A person's house is regarded as their territory. People talk of 'homesickness' when they miss being at home.

People may be judged from where they live, the type of house they live in, whether it is owned or rented. So housing is much more than just bricks and mortar.

During the Second World War, when many thousands of homes were damaged or destroyed, local authorities took the opportunity to clear away the slums and build new homes. In many instances, they replaced this poor housing with high-rise blocks of flats. The flats were generally of a higher standard than the housing they replaced. For the first time people had good sanitation, bathrooms and hot and cold water.

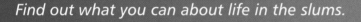

> *Find out what you can about life in the slums.*

However, moving families to the new flats and clearing the slums also meant destroying whole neighbourhoods and the feeling of community that existed in them. People who were moved often felt isolated and lonely, and missed the support of the extended family – brothers, sisters, grandparents, aunts and uncles.

Housing and health – Housing conditions are associated with health status in a number of ways. One obvious factor is inadequate heating, which can give rise to hypothermia, where the temperature of the body falls abnormally low, in the old and very young. Overcrowding may cause <u>respiratory</u> diseases and may also contribute to mental illness. The homes of managers and professionals are likely to possess more amenities than those of unskilled workers.

THE JARGON DRAGON

respiratory – breathing

Can living in high-rise flats affect your health and well-being?

The homes of higher paid workers are likely to have more amenities than those of unskilled workers

As many as two million dwellings in England are considered unfit for people to live in because they lack basic amenities such as a shower or bath, or may require repairs. They are also likely to be in areas where the air is polluted with industrial waste. These dwellings are likely to be inhabited by unskilled workers.

Think IT THROUGH

In a group, come up with a list of amenities you would expect to find in a modern house.

?

Unemployment

People with little or no money may not be able to pay for food or heating. Children and older people, in particular, need good, nourishing food for their physical development, such as bone formation. As we have seen above, inadequate heating can lead to serious health problems.

Some groups are particularly vulnerable to becoming unemployed, such as those already on low wages. One survey of unemployed men found that as many as half had been receiving the lowest earnings in the national earning distribution. There is clear evidence that there is a high rate of unemployment among young people, older workers, those in poor health, and women.

> *Find out what the phrase 'national earning distribution' means.*

The effects of unemployment on health and well-being – Unemployment also affects people's ability to pay for leisure activities, possibly leading to depression and ill-health. Unemployed people are more likely to live in crowded, cheaper housing, where damp conditions and environmental pollution (see page 116) may cause health problems.

Researchers suggest that the loss of a job is comparable to bereavement. Many unemployed people, for example, experience feelings of hopelessness, self-blame, sadness, lack of energy, loss of self-esteem and self-confidence, insomnia, suicidal thoughts and an increased use of tobacco and alcohol. People react to unemployment in different ways depending on:

- the availability of work in the future
- the individual's feelings about the circumstances surrounding the loss of the job (for example, does the unemployed person feel the victim of circumstances and not personally responsible?)
- the response of spouse, children and relatives
- the sense of 'loss of face' or respect in the community
- the financial implications
- the extent of supportive networks in the community.

Many unemployed people experience significantly fewer positive feelings, and more strain, anxiety and depression. Becoming employed again very quickly restores well-being.

The effects of unemployment upon health, however, are not at all clear. Some studies indicate that unemployment may be a factor in poor health. Studies have also found high levels of stress among unemployed people. Unskilled people and who have been unemployed for long periods tend to have higher blood pressure and also tend to be fatter than those people in the professional class. They are also more likely to suffer from arthritis, angina, respiratory problems, alcohol-related disease and mental illness.

Environmental pollution

The influence of the local environment on the health and well-being of individuals and groups has long been recognised. In the 19th century the health needs of people living in growing cities like Manchester or London prompted major programmes to improve water supplies and sewerage. These changes were a major factor in the decline of infectious disease.

Today some environments can still cause serious disease, for example the existence of asbestos or lead can cause damage to health.

Environmental factors	Effect upon health and well-being
Poor quality water Dirty, untreated	Gastric upsets
Contaminated with micro-organisms	Dysentery Hepatitis
Excessive levels of chemicals, e.g. nitrates	Typhoid Cholera
Inadequate sewerage	
Poor drainage treatment Old drains that need replacing	Water-borne infections, such as gastro-enteritis, dysentery, hepatitis, typhoid, polio, cholera
Untreated sewage getting into water supply Untreated sewage in areas where people bathe	
Inadequate refuse disposal	
Poor facilities for collecting rubbish Lack of proper refuse disposal sites	Infestations of rats and mice, causing food poisoning (and possibly Weil's disease, a rare jaundice spread in rats' urine), flies, causing gastro-enteritis, dysentery, typhoid, cholera

Community health and hygiene – Nowadays we expect:

- good quality housing
- good town planning
- clean, wholesome water
- clear air clean, safe food
- effective sewage disposal
- effective refuse disposal
- clean cities and towns
- unspoiled country and coastal areas
- clean milk
- high levels of vaccination to prevent outbreaks of infectious diseases.

Ways of measuring physical health

This section will help you understand indicators of health and how they can be measured, and how these measures can be taken and used to find out the state of a person's physical health. You will also learn that a person's age, sex and how they live have to be taken into account when interpreting the measurement that is recorded.

Blood pressure

Blood pressure describes the amount of pressure that the blood exerts on the walls of the arteries as it flows through them. It is an important measurement because it can give clues as to the state of a person's arteries.

Blood pressure is recorded in two figures – the upper figure is the systolic. This is the pressure in the blood vessels when the heart contracts. The lower figure, the diastolic, is the pressure when the heart is relaxing between beats. The systolic pressure is usually between 110 and 140 and the diastolic pressure between 75 and 80.

This is written down as: $\dfrac{110}{75}$

Using a traditional sphygmomanometer to measure blood pressure

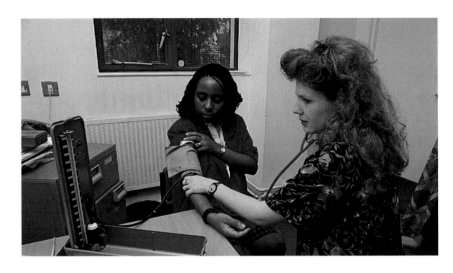

Measuring blood pressure

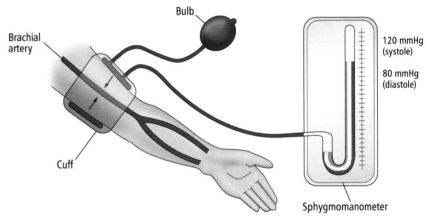

The most common way to measure blood pressure is as follows:

- The bell of a stethoscope is placed over the brachial artery.
- The sphygmomanometer cuff is wrapped around the arm above the elbow.
- The cuff is inflated and mercury rises up the manometer, from which the pressure is read.

The cuff is inflated approximately 20–30mmHg (mercury) above the last recorded reading, or until the pulse can no longer be heard.

The pressure valve is used to deflate the cuff slowly. The first sound to be heard through the stethoscope is the systolic reading and the point at which the pulse can be heard to fade is the diastolic reading.

Blood pressure varies with age, weight, race, socio-economic status, physical activity and general health.

About one in three people aged over 50 have raised blood pressure.

Mary is 14. Her older brother Ken is unemployed. They live on an old-style housing estate surrounded by factories and near to a motorway. They live with their mum, dad and grandmother in a three-bedroomed house. Ken has to sleep on the settee in the living-room so that his sister and grandmother can each have a room of their own.

Mary suffers from asthma and has an hour's journey to the nearest hospital when she has a serious attack. Her doctor is also a 20-minute bus trip away. Pollution from the factories and the motorway traffic contribute to her asthma attacks.

Ken is finding it difficult to get full-time work; he cannot afford to run a car and the local public transport is very infrequent and expensive.

Mary and Ken's mum works part-time in a local pub and their dad has been unemployed since the closure of the factory that he worked in. He is under treatment for depression and feels that no one wants to employ him at the age of 56. He hangs about the house all day, smokes heavily, does no exercise and is beginning to put on weight.

Q *What social factors could contribute to Mary's health and well-being?*

What are the physical factors that contribute to Mary's health and well-being?

What emotional factor is contributing to the depression of Ken and Mary's father?

Peak flow

Various measurements are taken of lung capacity. Vital capacity refers to the volume of air breathed out after a person has breathed in as fully as possible. The normal capacity is approximately 2500–3000ml. It is higher in males than females. Forced vital capacity measurements are taken in the form of peak flow measurement. Vital capacity is reduced in obstructive lung diseases, such as bronchitis, which is inflammation of the bronchi. A person suffering from asthma would also have a reduced vital capacity, due to difficulty in expiration because of the muscular spasm of the bronchi.

FIND IT OUT

Look in a book on biology to discover where the bronchi are.

Lung volume

The measurement of air taken into and expelled from the lungs is **spirometry**. Changes in lung volumes provide the best measurement of obstruction to air flow in the respiratory passages.

Using a spirometer

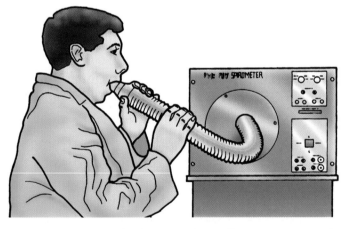

A spirometer consists of a hollow drum floating over a chamber of water and counterbalanced by weights so that it can move freely up and down. Inside the drum is a mixture of gases, usually oxygen and air. Leading from the hollow space in the drum to the outside is a tube that has a mouthpiece through which the patient breathes. As the patient inhales and exhales through the tube, the drum rises and falls, causing a needle to move on a nearby rotating chart. The tracing recorded is called a spirogram.

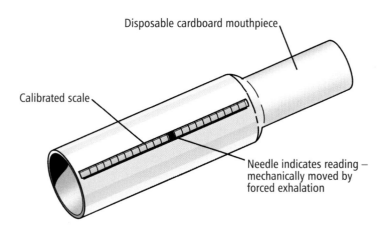

Disposable cardboard mouthpiece

Calibrated scale

Needle indicates reading – mechanically moved by forced exhalation

A peak flow meter

Body mass index

We are all familiar with our own body size and shape. Looking around we can see there is an immense variation in others' sizes and shapes. We are all individuals. If, however, a person is under-weight, this can be an indicator of their physical health. The body mass index is often used to measure this aspect of health.

Body mass index (BMI) can be calculated by dividing a person's weight (in kilograms) by the square of their height (in metres). This can then be used as a guide to five BMI groups:

Underweight: BMI 19.9 and below
Normal: BMI 20–24.9
Grade 1 obesity: BMI 25–29.9
Grade 2 obesity: BMI 30–39.9
grade 3 obesity: BMI 40 and above.

Average or normal

It is important to remember that it is possible to be different from the average in height, weight, length, etc., but still be within normal limits.

Weight – The average weight for a newborn baby is 3.5kg (7lb 11 oz). The heaviest recorded live-born baby weighed in at 9.3kg (20lb 8oz)!

Babies should be weighed regularly, as weight gain and contentment are signs that they are being fed adequately. A baby can be expected to double his or her birth weight in the first six months, and treble it by the end of the first year.

Children (and adults) will become fat if they overeat and do not have enough exercise. They can tend to overeat if they are worried, bored or insecure. It is unwise to give a small child too many sweets or fattening foods. Excessive weight gain in the early years makes it more likely that a child will be overweight in later life.

Average heights and weights from birth to 5 years

Age	Weight		Height	
	kg	lb	cm	in
Girls				
Birth	3.4	7.5	53.0	20.9
3 months	5.6	12.3		
6 months	6.9	15.2		
9 months	8.7	19.2		
1 year	9.7	21.4	74.2	29.2
2 years	12.2	26.9	85.6	33.7
3 years	14.3	31.5	93.0	36.6
4 years	16.3	35 9	100.4	39.5
5 years	18.3	40.3	107.2	42.4
Boys				
Birth	3.5	7.7	54.0	21.3
3 months	5.9	13.1		
6 months	7.9	17.4		
9 months	9.2	20.3		
1 year	10.2	22.5	76.3	30.0
2 years	12.7	28.0	86.9	34.2
3 years	14.7	32.4	94.2	37.1
4 years	16.6	36.6	101.6	40.0
5 years	18.5	40.7	108.3	42.6

Height – The average length of a new baby is 50cm. By the second birthday, children are likely to have reached half their eventual adult height.

Parents or carers must not become preoccupied with a child's size. If a child is happy, contented, growing and energetic there is nothing to worry about.

Resting pulse rate and recovery after exercise

Measuring the pulse

Each time the heart beats to pump blood, a wave passes along the walls of the arteries. This wave is the pulse and it can be felt at any point in the body where a large artery crosses a bone just beneath the skin.

The pulse is usually counted at the radial artery in the wrist (see page 124) or the carotid artery in the neck.

To take a pulse, the fingertips (but not the thumb tips) are placed over the site where the pulse is being taken. The beats

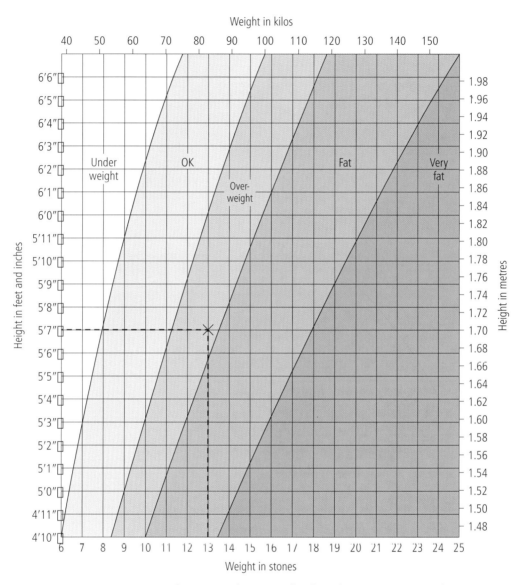

Weight in kilos

Height in feet and inches

Height in metres

Weight in stones

- - - - -   For example, a person who is 5'7" tall and weighs 13 stones is overweight

This graph shows the heights and weights of adults. To find out whether you need to lose or gain weight, draw a line up from your weight and across from your height. Mark a cross where the two meet

are counted for a full minute and then recorded. Normally the rhythm is regular and the volume is sufficient to make the pulse easily felt.

The three main observations, which are made on the pulse, are rate, rhythm and strength.

The average adult pulse rate varies between 60 and 80 beats per minute, while a young baby has a heart rate of about 140 beats per minute.

An increased pulse rate may indicate recent exercise, emotion, infection, blood or fluid loss, shock and heart disease.

Taking the radial pulse

Ways of promoting and supporting health improvement

This section will help you understand why measuring a person's health and setting targets is important before a health improvement plan can be produced. You will learn how realistic health improvement targets can be made for others. You will also understand how different health behaviours can help people achieve health improvement targets.

Before you undertake any health improvement plan, you should understand the benefits of a healthy lifestyle. These can be summarised as follows:

- Increased mobility as a result of increased exercise and an improved diet. Weight loss may improve your flexibility and mobility, while weight gain (if you are underweight) may increase your general energy level and again improve your mobility.
- Improved self-esteem. If you do something about the phrase 'I'm too fat/thin/unfit/etc.', you will feel better about yourself.
- Reduced risks to health, particularly those that show up in later life. The big killers of middle age, namely heart disease and smoking-related diseases, often come from poor habits in earlier years. Changes to your diet, exercise routines and other habits at an early age will be beneficial in later life.

Monitoring your recreational activities may help you to identify possible dangers to your well-being that can be addressed now. Habits are easier to establish than they are to get rid of.

Motivating individuals to improve their health

People do not readily respond to being preached at about their health, so it is necessary to involve them in setting health improvement plans for themselves.

The aims of such plans should be:

- the **empowerment** of the individual so that they can make choices based on information
- to bring about changes in their behaviour (for example stopping smoking or drinking less)
- to give them information and increase their awareness of health issues that affect them.

THE JARGON DRAGON

empowerment – allowing people to make decisions for themselves

Information and choice

Information is the first step towards making healthy choices. Consider how healthy you are. You know how unpleasant it is to feel unwell, but what does being healthy really mean? A person who is in good health is someone whose body is working at maximum efficiency, both mentally and physically.

Before embarking on any health programme, an individual will usually have their personal fitness assessed against standards and have their health checked by a doctor.

Checks against physical fitness will include:

- height
- weight
- blood pressure
- pulse
- muscular strength
- body measurements (chest, waist, hips, thighs, biceps etc.)
- lung efficiency.

Measuring physical fitness

There are many tests that have been devised to measure physical fitness. Many involve detailed measurements and calculations. The activity described below will give you some idea of the level of exercise that will help you to improve your health.

(**Warning:** Do not attempt to carry out this activity if you know you have any breathing difficulties or heart disease. The activities are not dangerous, but it would be best to get medical advice about exercise routines.)

- Work with a partner so that you can measure each other's pulse rate. You will need a watch with a second hand.
- Together decide what you consider to be gentle exercise. (This may be as simple as walking steadily up some stairs.)
- Before you start, measure your resting heart rate by counting the heartbeats for 15 seconds using the pulse found in your wrist. Multiply the answer by four to get the beats per minute. Record this figure as the resting pulse.
- Carry out your gentle exercise for 1 minute. Then record your heartbeat at 1-minute intervals until it gets back to the resting rate.
- Repeat the activity for longer periods of 2, 5 and 10 minutes (or possibly longer), until it takes more than 5 minutes for your pulse to return to its resting rate.
- The last but one activity level is the amount of exercise you should start off doing. This means that you should start with the period of exercising that requires 5 minutes for your pulse to return to normal. The heart rate achieved is a guide as to the level you should work to.
- Using the result as a guide, start a programme of exercises three or four times a week. At the end of each exercise session, measure your maximum heart rate and the time taken to return to the resting rate.
- Increase the amount of exercise to reach your maximum pulse that still returns to normal after 5 minutes' rest. You should find that you are able to exercise more as you get fitter.

(**Note:** The maximum heart rate that you should not exceed is calculated by subtracting your age from 220:

220 – your age = maximum heartbeats per minute

It is unlikely that you will approach this with the gentle exercises, but you should try to double your heartbeat during exercise.)

Exercise routines

Exercise routines can be divided into two types:

- Aerobic – exercise that works the heart, lungs and blood system, such as running, fast swimming and fast cycling.
- Anaerobic – exercise that concentrates on stretching and flexing the muscles, such as yoga and general stretch work.

A good exercise programme will combine the two types of exercise depending on individual needs.

Whichever activity is chosen, it is important to try to build up gradually. To gain and maintain a fitness level, aim for three 20-minute sessions per week. Exercise that is boring, gruelling or difficult to fit into their lifestyle will be a problem to maintain.

Questions to consider before undertaking exercise:

- Can you afford the cost of the exercise?
- Are you fit or do you need a medical check-up?
- Do you have suitable clothes and footwear?
- Is the weather suitable and safe for the exercise?
- Do you have enough time to warm up before and cool down after?
- Have you eaten enough and sufficiently early so that the food is digested?

Health promotion information, which can inform, motivate and support individuals when they are carrying out their health improvement plan, can be found in the following forms:

- leaflets
- models
- posters
- videos
- advertisements
- displays
- games
- role-play activities
- slides
- magazine articles.

case study

Alice

Alice is 14. She is 1.70m (5ft 6in) tall and weighs 90kg (14 stone). She loves eating fast food and also eats snacks between meals. She does little physical exercise. Her doctor has told her she is overweight and has asked her to lose some weight.

She asks you to draw up a health improvement plan with her.

Q *How overweight is Alice? What other measurements would you need to know?*

What are the current risks to her health and well-being?

What else would you need to find out about Alice before you can draw up the plan with her?

Understanding personal

This unit will help you to:

understand the different ways in which people grow and develop during their life. It will help you find out about the process of human growth and development, and the different factors that can affect an individual's life experience.

development and relationships 3

In this unit you will learn about:

The stages and pattern of human growth and development

One useful way to study human development is to use the following headings:

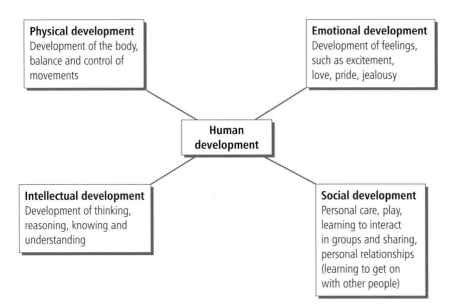

It is important to remember the difference between the terms 'growth' and 'development':

- growth refers to an increase in actual size of a person – in other words, their physical growth
- development means a person's increasing ability to master more complex skills, for example a child's ability to walk, talk or manipulate things with the fingers.

Becoming taller is an obvious growth, while a baby's ability to reach for objects or transfer them from one hand to another shows a development of complex skills.

We have already seen in Unit 2 that when looking at personal development we must also consider certain basic needs. These are physical, emotional, social and intellectual needs.

Development and growth: what is the difference?

Physical needs	Shelter Security and rest	Protection Prevention of illness or injury	Fresh air and sunlight Training in life skills
Emotional needs	Affection Dignity and self-respect	Play	Personal identity
Social needs	Relationships Groups	Friends	Family

Intellectual needs	Thinking skills
	Remembering
	Using words
		Continuous individual
		  care
		Opportunity to learn from
		  experience
			Problem solving
			Teachers

There are five main life stages of human development:

Infancy	0–3 years
Childhood	4–10 years
Adolescence	11–18 years
Adulthood	19–65 years
Later adulthood	65+ years

We will now look at each stage of life in turn.

Infancy 0–3 years

Personal development begins at birth. The sequence (or order) of development is roughly the same for all children, but the rate (or speed) of development will vary from child to child. The parts of the body near the brain develop first. For example, active use of the mouth, the eyes and hearing come before sitting, walking and the use of fingers. The table on pages 136–7 shows the areas of development from 0–3 years.

FIND IT OUT

> *What is your earliest memory?*

When a baby is born, one of the first questions a mother may well ask is 'Is my baby normal?'. To check that all is well, a number of tests are carried out on the baby:

- the airway and palate of the mouth are examined
- tests assess the baby's heart rate, breathing and reflexes
- the baby's hips are checked to see that they are not dislocated
- head size and birth weight are recorded
- skin colour is observed – new babies may be jaundiced, where they appear yellow in colour.

Average features of a newborn baby

Average weight   3.5kg (7.7lb)
Average length   50cm
Average head size   33–35cm

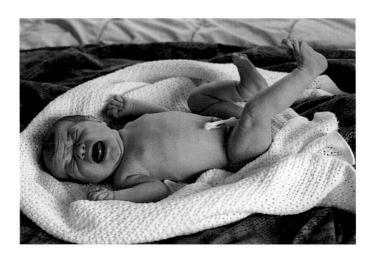

The newborn baby is helpless

Human babies are very helpless and their growth is very slow, compared to other animals. New human babies cry to attract their mother's attention and after a few weeks will smile and show pleasure when their parents appear. The table below summarises human development in the first three years.

Children are generally referred to as infants in their first year and as toddlers in their second and third years.

Which of the following are physical and which are social developments?

- *Stands when supported.*
- *Plays 'peek-a-boo'.*
- *Spoon-feeds without spilling.*
- *Throws a small ball.*

FIND IT OUT

Childhood 4–10 years

Between the ages of 4 and 10, children become increasingly active and communicative. This section describes the different areas of development for this stage.

Physical development

During this period children continue to develop and perfect many of the physical skills, which have been acquired since birth. Skills include:

- running
- walking
- climbing
- riding a tricycle
- sitting cross-legged
- moving in time with music
- playing ball games.

Development from birth to three years

Age	Physical development	Intellectual development	Emotional development	Social development
1 month	Holds head erect for a few seconds. Eyes follow a moving light	Interested in sounds	Cries in response to pain, hunger and thirst	May sleep up to 20 hours in a 24-hour period. Stops crying when picked up and spoken to
3 months	Eyes follow a person moving. Kicks vigorously	Recognises carer's face. Shows excitement. Listens, smiles, holds rattle	Enjoys being cuddled and played with. Misses carer and cries for carer to return	Responds happily to carer. Becomes excited at prospect of a feed or bath
6 months	Able to lift head and chest up supported by wrists. Turns to a person who is speaking	Responds to speech. Vocalises. Uses eyes a lot. Holds toys. Explores using hands. Listens to sound	Can be anxious in presence of strangers. Can show anger and frustration. Shows a clear preference for mother's company	Puts everything in mouth. Plays with hands and feet. Tries to hold bottle when feeding
9 months	Stands when supported. May crawl. Gazes at self in mirror	Tries to hold drinking cup. Sits without support	Tries to talk, babbling. May say 'Mama' and 'Dada'. Shouts for attention. Understands 'No'. Still anxious about strangers. Sometimes irritable if routine is altered	Can recognise individuals – mother, father, siblings. Plays 'Peek-a-boo'. Imitates hand clapping. Puts hands round cup when feeding
12 months	Pulls self up to standing position. Uses pincer grip. Feeds self using fingers. May walk without assistance	Knows own name. Obeys simple instructions. Says about three words	Shows affection. Gives kisses and cuddles. Likes to see familiar faces but less worried by strangers	Drinks from a cup without assistance. Holds a spoon but cannot feed self. Plays 'Pat-a-cake'. Quickly finds hidden toys
1–1½ years	Walks well, feet apart. Runs carefully. Pushes and pulls large toys. Walks upstairs. Creeps backwards downstairs	Uses 6–20 recognisable words. Repeats last word of short sentences. Enjoys and tries to join in with nursery rhymes. Picks up named toys. Enjoys looking at simple picture books. Builds a tower of 3–4 bricks. Scribbles and makes dots. Preference for right or left hand shown	Affectionate, but may still be reserved with strangers. Likes to see familiar faces	Able to hold spoon and to get food into mouth. Holds drinking cup and hands it back when finished. Can take off shoes and socks. Bowel control may have been achieved. Remembers where objects belong

Age	Physical development	Intellectual development	Emotional development	Social development
2 years	Runs on whole foot. Squats steadily. Climbs on furniture. Throws a small ball. Sits on a small tricycle and moves vehicle with feet	Uses 50 or more recognisable words; understands many more words; puts two or three words together to form simple sentences. Refers to self by name. Asks names of objects and people. Scribbles in circles. Can build a tower of six or seven cubes. Hand preference is obvious	Can display negative behaviour and resistance. May have temper tantrums if thwarted. Plays contentedly beside other children but not with them. Constantly demands mother's attention	Asks for food and drink. Spoon feeds without spilling. Puts on shoes
2–2½ years	All locomotive skills now improving. Runs and climbs. Able to jump from a low step with feet together. Kicks a large ball	May use 200 or more words. Knows full name. Continually asking questions, likes stories and recognises details in picture books. Recognises self in photographs. Builds a tower of seven or more cubes	Usually active and restless. Emotionally still very dependent on adults. Tends not to want to share playthings	Eats skilfully with a spoon and may sometimes use a fork. Active and restless. Often dry through the day
3 years	Sits with feet crossed at ankles. Walks upstairs with one foot on each step	Able to state full name, sex and sometimes age. Carries on simple conversations and constantly questioning. Demands favourite story over and over again. Can count to 10 by rote. Can thread wooden beads on string. Can copy a circle and a cross. Names colours. Cuts with scissors. Paints with a large brush	Becomes less prone to temper tantrums. Affectionate and confiding, showing affection for younger siblings. Begins to understand sharing	Eats with a fork and spoon. May be dry through the night

Perfecting new skills

Children aged around 5 appear taller and slimmer than toddlers and their features have a more adult look. Movements are well co-ordinated and physical skill increases. The growth rate follows a steady, but slower, pattern until the age of puberty ends at about 18 years of age. Girls tend to develop more quickly than boys, both physically and intellectually.

Intellectual development

Children from the age of about 4 begin to speak grammatically (using words in their proper place), recount recent events accurately, enjoy jokes and are able to state their name, address, age and birthday.

Children at this stage begin to develop a greater capacity for directed thinking

Ask your parents how old you were when you were first able to give the date of your birthday when asked.

From the age of 4, children will also be gaining control in writing and drawing. A recognisable person may be drawn, such as father or mother, also a house that has doors, windows and a roof. Pictures are coloured neatly and four or more primary colours can be named.

Children at this stage begin to develop a greater capacity for **directed thinking**. This means that they develop the ability to concentrate on one task and finish it.

Children who have never been separated from their parents before may experience problems of adjustment when they start school. They may be unable to settle and as a result cry, become aggressive or angry. Carers working with children of this age should be sensitive to this possibility.

THE JARGON DRAGON

directed thinking – the ability to concentrate on one thing

Think about your own first day at school and your feelings at that time. Discuss in a group what your reactions were and the reasons for them.

Think IT THROUGH

From the age of about 4, pictures are coloured neatly

Emotional development

By the age of 5 or 6 years, children are able to use a fork, spoon and knife. They can dress and undress themselves, although they may have some difficulty with fastenings, such as buttons and shoelaces. They indulge in make-believe play and in general are more sensitive. They relate clock time to their daily programmes of events. They will know when they have their dinner or tea and the time they usually go to bed.

Children of this age need the companionship of other children and begin to develop personal relationships. They gradually become more independent from their parents. They will play with other children and also by themselves. They will comfort playmates who are upset, choose their own friends, begin to understand the rules of games and understand what is fair play. At about 5 years of age, a child will usually start to attend school.

Towards the end of the childhood stage, between about the ages of 7 and 10, life revolves around the family, school and the community. Independence is increasing and variations in children's abilities to do different things become more obvious.

During this stage of development, children continue to experience the growth of feelings about themselves and others. They also begin to develop their self-image and identity (how they see themselves).

By the age of 10, childhood is nearly finished and puberty is beginning. The skills of 10-year-old children bring together all that has been experienced and learned in childhood, in school, with family and with friends.

Social development

Up to the age of about 4, children relate first to their mother and then to their father, brothers, sisters and other relations. This range of contacts grows when school starts.

In school, the teacher may take on the role of parents in the children's eyes, but the teacher cannot give undivided attention to every child. Sometimes, therefore, children who are used to a lot of individual attention from their parents may find it difficult to adjust to school at first.

The teacher may take on the role of parents

Between the ages of 4 and 10, girls tend to develop more rapidly than boys, both physically and intellectually. Boys tend not to play with or develop relationships with girls at this stage. Boys will tend to play football, 'rough and tumble' games and other activities in groups, while girls will have their own activities and games.

By the time children reach the age of 9, special friendships will have been developed. However, 9-year-old children can be very critical of each other and may exclude some individuals from their games. You will see this in any school playground.

Adolescence 11–18 years

Adolescence is the name given to the period of life between the onset of puberty at about 11 to the beginning of adult life at 18.

Adolescence coincides with a growth spurt. It is a time of social and biological change. Adolescence is also a period when a lot of intellectual and emotional changes occur. Adolescents have to grow physically into a new body. They also have to come to terms with new feelings and attitudes.

Physical development

Puberty literally means 'age of adulthood'. Physical changes occur because of increased production of the sex hormones oestrogen in girls and testosterone in boys.

THE JARGON DRAGON

puberty – the 'age of manhood', when physical changes occur to the body as a result of the increased production of sex hormones

Oestrogen is produced in the ovaries in girls. Testosterone is produced in the testes in boys. These hormones cause the development of bones, hair and genital organs.

Puberty in girls – Changes in girls tend to start at 10 to 12 years of age, sometimes even earlier. These include:

- a growth spurt
- breast development
- appearance of pubic and armpit hair
- broadening of the hips
- a redistribution of fat
- menstruation (periods).

Puberty in boys – In boys, the changes associated with puberty usually start at 12 to 14 years. These include:

- a growth spurt
- facial hair
- deepening of the voice
- enlargement of the penis, scrotum and testes
- appearance of pubic, chest and armpit hair
- the limbs lengthen and shoulders become broader
- the ability to ejaculate.

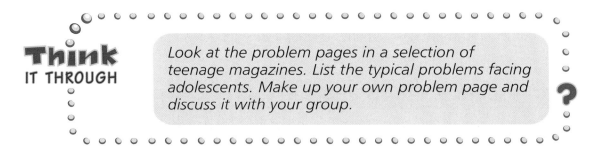

Think IT THROUGH

Look at the problem pages in a selection of teenage magazines. List the typical problems facing adolescents. Make up your own problem page and discuss it with your group.

Hormonal changes can lead adolescent boys and girls to develop spots. This can develop into acne (a more serious, unsightly skin condition). Although it is distressing, it is a normal part of growing up and is treatable.

Intellectual development

Adolescents begin to think about themselves and what others think about them. They begin to compare the ideal world with what they experience in reality, in terms of families, politics and religion.

They will experiment with different identities. For example, they may try being a punk, a hippie or a rebel and in extreme cases delinquent or criminal behaviour may be the result. Many of these identities may be the opposite of what their parents are or want for them. Some level of role-playing may not be a bad thing. It allows adolescents to achieve their personal identity.

Adolescence is also a time when people start to think about the future – a possible career, a committed relationship or going on to university, for example.

? *Do you think you have developed intellectually? Have you thought about the future? Do you have a plan for the future?*

Think
IT THROUGH

What do adolescents say about this period in their life?

Emotional development

Adolescents often experience mood swings and feelings of ambivalence. This means that they may feel one thing about a person or subject one day and another the next day. For example, sometimes they may co-operate with their parents, but at other times they may refuse to co-operate. Parents and friends may be confused by such behaviour. They may not understand what adolescents are thinking or feeling. Relationships between parents and children often become very difficult at this stage.

Social development

Adolescence is a time when a person is neither a child nor an adult. However, it is also a time when interest in sex begins.

Many of the issues associated with adolescence are **psycho-social** in nature. For example, spots are physical things but they may also cause psycho-social problems such as depression, shyness, embarrassment, and prevent a person socialising and developing personal relationships.

It is also a time when a person's individual identity (their own **personality**) becomes established. Moral (right and wrong), social and personal responsibilities are also developed. Adolescents often do this by challenging accepted ways of behaving. By rebelling against their parents or teachers, they are testing and developing their own ideas of what is right and wrong.

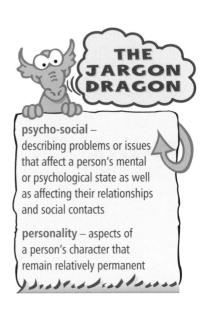

THE JARGON DRAGON

psycho-social – describing problems or issues that affect a person's mental or psychological state as well as affecting their relationships and social contacts

personality – aspects of a person's character that remain relatively permanent

Intimate relationships develop at this stage

Adulthood 19–65 years

During adulthood most people reach the peak of their performance, with skeletal growth being complete in the late teens or early twenties. From the age of 30 years or so signs of ageing begin to show.

During childhood and adolescence the individual is dependent upon others. During adulthood, however, individuals are expected to take responsibility for themselves, and for children, for their own old age and perhaps for the care of older people.

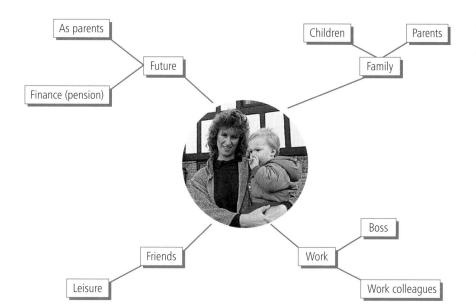

As parents — Future — Finance (pension)

Children — Family — Parents

Friends — Leisure

Work — Boss — Work colleagues

Adults are required to take responsibility for themselves and others may be dependent upon them

The 19–25-year-old adult

People in this group are at the beginning of adult life. They may still be involved in education or training. Perhaps they are at university or college and still receiving financial support in the form of grants, loans or assistance from parents.

In addition, they may have left the family home and be living in a different part of the country. They may be considering home ownership.

They may be employed or unemployed and receiving state benefits. This can be a time of freedom, providing financial stability has been achieved.

Peolple in this age group may settle down as a couple in a committed relationship

People in this age group may also be considering settling down as a couple and starting a family. The process of becoming a 'couple' will tend to follow a certain path:

- first, there is the single-sex group within which social activities occur
- then mixed groups start to form
- girls and boys begin to take an interest in forming relationships with each other
- for girls, the approval of boys becomes more important than acceptance by their girlfriends
- mixed groups of couples appear, but later individual couples dominate the social scene
- couples may develop an interest in sexual relationships, hopefully within a framework of respect and caring
- individuals begin to explore their own sexual identity and may form gay relationships.

The 25–40-year-old adult

This group is made up of men and women who may be married, in a relationship or single, with or without children. They may live as couples or single people.

If employed, they will usually be concentrating on their career, hoping to do well and improve their position and looking for promotion. Many job adverts in magazines and newspapers are looking for people in this age group, because they have some experience, yet are still energetic and ambitious.

By the time people are in their late twenties they have often formed a steady relationship. They may get engaged, get married or decide to live together as a couple in a stable relationship. Many relationships end in separation or divorce, but there are still many couples enjoying a happy and loving relationship.

During this stage, couples and single parents will be bringing up a family, with the need for a reasonable income, housing and community facilities to help them to do so.

Identify two life changes that a person in adulthood could experience. Discuss the likely consequences of these changes.

FIND IT OUT

The 40–64-year-old adult

People in this age group (often called 'middle age') may have experienced a career change, may have taken early retirement or may have been made redundant.

Middle age can be a time to feel confident, relaxed and able to enjoy life

Children of people in this age group will often be growing up and starting their own families and careers.

Middle age can be a time of greater security in life. People will have brought up their own children, have greater financial security and will have achieved some, if not all, of their career goals. It should be a time to feel confident, relaxed and able to enjoy life.

However, people sometimes feel negative during this life stage. They may feel, perhaps, that they have lost the main role in their life (bringing up children). They may be faced with the prospect of caring for elderly relatives just when they would like to enjoy some independence. Dissatisfaction with achievements or lack of recognition at work can also cause concern.

People in this age group may experience some of the early symptoms of ageing, such as grey hair, long-sightedness and dental problems. Ill-health also becomes more common. People are more likely to die in this age group as a result of heart disease, cancer and respiratory disorders.

Women begin to experience the menopause (known as the 'change of life') any time after the age of 40. This involves a series of changes in hormones, including the end of menstruation, which eventually means the end of a woman's ability to have children.

The parents of people in this age group will be becoming elderly and possibly dependent on their children.

Later adulthood 65 years+

Later adulthood is often viewed in a negative way – as a stage of life that just brings problems, such as the need for residential accommodation or health and social care. But people do not change simply because they have reached old age. They continue with their life in the same way they have always done. Many remain independent for most, if not all, of their life.

Later adulthood can be divided into two stages:

- up to 75 years old
- beyond 75 years.

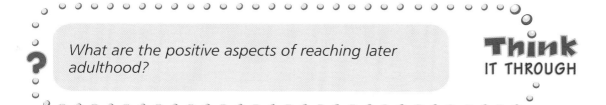

? *What are the positive aspects of reaching later adulthood?*

Think IT THROUGH

With increased life expectancy, people may have 30 years or more in 'retirement'

Today, people are living longer than ever before. About 18 per cent of the population of the UK are now over retirement age (this is regarded as being 65). Women tend to outlive men by about five years on average. The length of time a person can expect to live in years is known as life expectancy. Things that can affect **life expectancy** include:

THE JARGON DRAGON

life expectancy – how long people can be expected to live

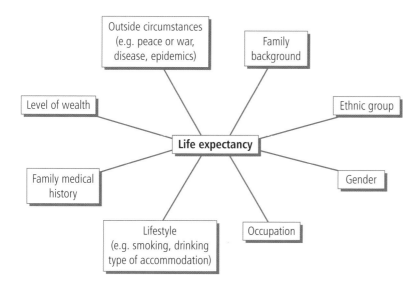

Outside circumstances (e.g. peace or war, disease, epidemics)

Family background

Level of wealth

Ethnic group

Life expectancy

Family medical history

Gender

Lifestyle (e.g. smoking, drinking type of accommodation)

Occupation

Life expectancy

Look through a selection of newspapers and magazines and find positive images of older people.

The physical changes that can occur in later adulthood

Some of the physical changes that are happening throughout life and may become more obvious in later adulthood include the following:

Skin – dryness, wrinkling and loss of elasticity.

Hair – growth slows, thinning occurs, men may go bald and all body hair goes grey.

Eyesight – long-sightedness may develop. People find it harder to distinguish colours. Changing from bright light to dark becomes a problem. Side vision becomes more narrow. Cataracts and glaucoma can lead to blindness if left untreated.

Hearing – the ability to hear deteriorates. Appreciation of high-pitched frequencies is lost first.

Smell and taste – these senses deteriorate, sometimes causing loss of appetite.

Teeth – may deteriorate quite early in life. Gum disease and decay can become major problems.

The lungs and respiratory system – the lungs become less elastic and respiratory muscles weaken. Older people are more likely to be affected by physical disorders.

The heart and blood vessels – the efficiency of the heart decreases. Blood vessels become less elastic and blood pressure may be raised.

The digestive system – secretions of saliva and digestive juices decrease with age. Food takes much longer to pass through the body as muscles become weaker and less effective. Constipation can then become a problem.

The urinary system – the kidneys become less efficient at filtering out waste products effectively.

The reproductive system – in women the menopause will have marked the end of reproductive life.

The skeleton and muscles – between the ages of 20 and 70 a person can lose 5cm (2in) in height. Total bone mass is reduced and muscles become less flexible. Posture and mobility are likely to be altered considerably.

This all sounds negative. There is no denying that certain aspects of the ageing process can be very troublesome to some individuals, but for most people the inconveniences are not serious.

Other changes in later adulthood

Personality – It is often said that old people do not like change. Like most people in fact, elderly people find familiar surroundings and situations a comfort.

Memory – You may notice that some elderly people easily forget what has happened recently, but clearly remember things that have happened several decades ago. This may be because of the way the memory works – earlier events are imprinted on the brain by repetition (the person may have experienced a particular event a number of times). The brain remembers these earlier events better than more recent events.

Learning and intelligence – Older people do tend to take longer to absorb new information than younger people, but they do not become less intelligent. Many older people take Open University degrees or enrol in classes in local colleges.

Look up the meaning of the word 'intelligence'.

FIND IT OUT

Social aspects of later adulthood
The main social aspects of later adulthood are:

- retirement
- family changes
- loneliness
- changing roles.

Retirement – When people leave work they feel that they lose their status in society. They no longer have a job to do outside the home. People may lose friendships, their income drops and their lifestyle changes.

Reduced income can give rise to problems. A retired person needs between 65 and 80 per cent of their previous income to maintain their standard of living at the same level. Most people's income drops by half and many drop by a lot more.

Adapting to life in retirement can be difficult for some people

Family changes – When their children have grown up, many older people become grandparents and great-grandparents. Older people have a considerable role to play in looking after their grandchildren, often in the form of child care and sometimes even by giving financial help.

Loneliness – Drastic changes are brought about when the life partner of an older person dies. The remaining partner may have little experience of financial matters. They may not drive or feel confident to attend functions by themselves or they may lack the ability to cook and care for themselves and their home.

People can be isolated in their own homes because of poor mobility or because they do not have many visitors or friends.

A surviving partner may have to cope with all the household chores

Janine is 19. She lives with her mother, Felicity, and father, Miles. Miles's elderly mother, Jessie, is 80 and also lives with the family.

Miles is the only person in the family who is working. His income is not adequate to support all of his family. Janine has had no support from her family with her studies. Her father was hoping that Janine might get a job when she left school, but she wants to go to university.

Jessie has lived in this house all her life. She lived in it with her husband until his death 20 years ago. Jessie lives in a flat on the ground floor of the house and seldom sees her son or his wife. Only Janine visits her every day and does little cleaning jobs for her. Jessie has a few old friends who visit her but she often feels lonely.

Q *How would Janine's leaving home affect the family?*

What physical changes could Jessie be experiencing?

The different factors that can affect human growth and development

Physical factors

Personal development

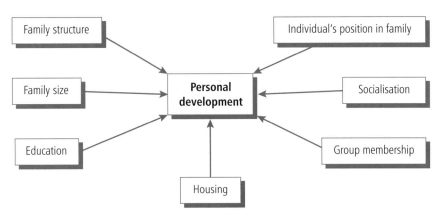

- Family structure
- Family size
- Education
- **Personal development**
- Housing
- Individual's position in family
- Socialisation
- Group membership

THE JARGON DRAGON

genetic inheritance – inheritance (or acquisition) of certain characteristics, such as eye or hair colour, from parents

Genetic inheritance

It is becoming more recognised that genes have an important part to play in the growth and development of individuals. Genes determine characteristics such as the colour of our eyes. Genes also affect our susceptibility to certain conditions such as cancer or heart disease. This is known as our **genetic inheritance**.

Diet

People from different groups are affected by what they eat or can afford to eat. People in lower socio-economic groups, who are on a low income, tend to eat food with low levels of dietary fibre. Research shows that babies' health is related to their mothers' health and nutritional intake.

Genes determine some of our physical characteristics

Why might people from lower income groups tend to eat food with low levels of dietary fibre?

Think
IT THROUGH

Illness or disease

Some people argue that people in the lower socio-economic groups have worse health because of poor habits, such as drinking, smoking and bad diet. People living in the north of England, for example, have been accused of eating too many stodgy foods to be good for them. This sort of comment is not helpful because it blames the victims for the situations they find themselves in, rather than looking at wider issues such as poverty, which is often the root of many problems to do with lifestyle. Comments such as these are described by psychologists as a **deficit model,** that is one that makes the victim out to be lacking in some way.

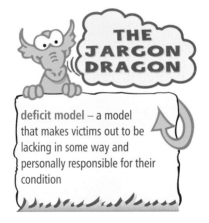

THE JARGON DRAGON

deficit model – a model that makes victims out to be lacking in some way and personally responsible for their condition

Further questions might be asked concerning what makes people lower down the social scale smoke or drink. What pressures are on them to resort to these things? What alternatives have they? Remember that limited income often means limited lifestyle.

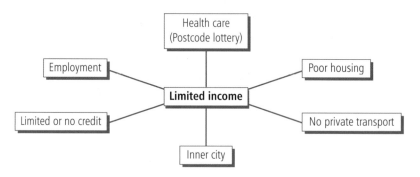

Limited income often means limited lifestyle

People from ethnic minority groups may also find it difficult to obtain the health care they need. Information may not be available in community languages, such as Punjabi or Urdu. There are other factors which might make it difficult for people to get care: transport may not be available to attend hospital appointments or the demands of other children may make it impossible to wait in long queues for antenatal checks.

Economic factors

Social class is a way of putting people into strata or layers, some higher than others. In the UK, the Registrar-General, a government official, collects information on all births, deaths and marriages, and census data every ten years.

See pages 163–5 for social and emotional factors.

FIND IT OUT

Find out what you can about the UK census. What kind of questions are asked?

Since the beginning of the 20th century, the Registrar-General has grouped people into a number of social classes, from a list of jobs, as a way of classifying people. The groupings are based on the income, status, skill and educational level of each job.

The government's social classification system

Class   Examples

Class	Examples
1	The Queen, large company owner
2	Company executive, manager of 25 people or more
3	Doctor, lawyer, scientist, teacher, librarian, IT engineer
4	Policeman, nurse, prison officer
5	Sales manager, farm manager
6	Office supervisor, civil servant, lab technician
7	Computer operator, dental nurse, secretary
8	Small-business owner with under 25 employees, publican
9	Self-employed bricklayer, driving instructor
10	Factory foreman, shop supervisor, senior hairdresser
11	Craft and related workers, plumber, mechanic
12–17	+other classifications + (un)skilled or unemployed

Income

Economic factors, such as the amount of income we have and how we spend it, affect how we live, and are linked to social class and employment or unemployment.

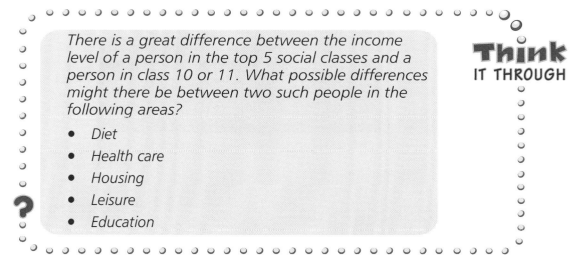

There is a great difference between the income level of a person in the top 5 social classes and a person in class 10 or 11. What possible differences might there be between two such people in the following areas?

- *Diet*
- *Health care*
- *Housing*
- *Leisure*
- *Education*

Think IT THROUGH

Of course, there are some individuals in the higher classes who lead a very unhealthy lifestyle and the opposite may be true for people in the lower classes.

Research has shown that children lower down the social scale tend to do less well educationally than those higher up. Think about the differences there may be between the groups in terms of role models (people you would like to copy), encouragement to go on to higher education, private education, extra tuition, a place to study and believing you can do it because you are expected to achieve.

Think IT THROUGH

Why are people with disabilities more likely to be less well off than able-bodied persons?

Why may people with disabilities find it difficult to get a job?

Environmental factors

Housing

We know that a home is a very significant factor in an individual's life. The place where we live can affect not only our physical health but also our mental health, and can even affect us socially. The effects are even greater if an individual doesn't have a home!

Think IT THROUGH

Consider the possible physical, emotional and social implications of living in bad housing, with cramped, damp conditions for the following people:

- a single parent with young children
- an elderly person living alone
- a teenager living with his or her family.

Thousands of people have no home, possibly because they have personal difficulties like alcoholism or mental health problems. Whatever the reason for their homelessness, one thing that is certain is that once they begin to live rough their health declines rapidly. The average age of death for a homeless person is 47 years.

Work

Working conditions can affect health. Think of the risk factors involved for those working in the building industry, refuse collection, steel factories, agriculture or with heavy industrial equipment.

Access to services

There is some evidence to suggest that there are more and better health services available in wealthy areas of the UK than in poorer areas. This means that people's access is limited if they live in one of these poorer areas. This is sometimes called the 'postcode lottery'.

How these factors can interrelate

Many of these factors are interrelated. This means that they are linked together. They can affect various aspects of a person's self-esteem, physical and mental health, employment prospects and level of education.

What does the term 'self-esteem' mean to you?

Economic factors affecting development

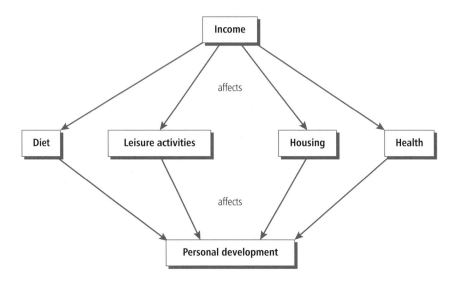

For example, if you lose your job you may become depressed, your self-esteem may become reduced and as a consequence you may not eat a proper diet, your health may deteriorate and your relationship may suffer.

The role of relationships in personal development

Family relationships

How early are relationships formed? The answer is early! No one really knows how early a baby notices its mother, father or main carer, the important point is that if a child is denied positive early relationships for a long time, this will affect the child's development. Babies who are neglected or ill-treated, who have had little stimulation, eye contact or physical contact, need a lot of help to become bright and affectionate themselves. Similarly, as the child grows, the relationship that develops gives the child a pattern for future relationships.

The influence of parents

Influential psychologists, such as Freud, Bowlby and Piaget, said that a child's early relationship with its parents (particularly the mother) sets the tone of later relationships. Children who have secure relationships with their parents are more likely to be

Children who have a secure relationship with their parents are more likely to be accepted by peers

accepted by their peers (meaning their friends and contemporaries). Sometimes children who have difficult relationships with brothers and sisters form closer friendships outside the home.

Find out who Freud, Bowlby and Piaget were.

FIND IT OUT

Nature and nurture – Parenting is a two-way process. It would be easy for parents if their children simply followed whatever their parents wanted them to do. Children, however, have a personality and will of their own so it is an interactive, or two-way, process. Two children in the same family can be very different even if their parents have brought them up in roughly the same way.

What does the phrase 'nature and nurture' mean?

FIND IT OUT

The influence of the family
Although the relationship between parent or main carer and child is a central one, other early relationships soon become significant. The relationship between brothers and sisters may be tempestuous at times, but they also provide many positive factors in the development of children.

Children can be very different even if their parents have brought them up the same way

In some cultures, for example, Islamic culture, the **extended family** (a family that includes grandparents, aunts, cousins) is very much alive. Today, in British society the **nuclear family** is more the norm. This family consists of a couple and their children living together, without members of the wider family. In many cases, relatives may be living far away from the nuclear family because of job commitments.

THE JARGON DRAGON

extended family – a family that includes grandparents, aunts, uncles and cousins, as well as parents and children

nuclear family – consists of a couple and their children living together, without members of their wider family

The extended family can provide a wide support group for a growing child

What are the consequences for the care of older people in cultures where nuclear families are the norm?

What are the consequences for the care of older people in cultures where nuclear families are the norm?

Other relationships

We saw in Unit 1 how people differ greatly in their need for close, informal or even formal relationships. There are those who like to spend long periods by themselves with no one else to be responsible for or to share their company with! Most people, however, need both informal relationships and more formal ones to thrive and be happy.

Formal or work relationships

Studies show that poor relationships at work are harmful to production and efficiency. Poor relationships at work can also lead to personal dissatisfaction, depression and ill-health for individuals. Many people would say that after the financial incentive to work the next incentive is the company they enjoy with their colleagues or workmates.

Thinking about your own experience at school, how significant are/were your relationships with your friends and teachers in terms of your motivation to attend school and learn?

In the learning environment, teachers also need to form relationships with those they teach to make the students' learning effective.

Social, informal relationships

Often we participate in relationships simply because we enjoy them. We may use our leisure time to play football or badminton. We may go to clubs and discos to meet with friends who are not associated with work, education or family. This is because we need to have a balanced life. We need to be free from the responsibilities of home and work for a short time to

Good formal relationships are important for success in our working lives

discover the lighter side of ourselves. We need to confirm aspects of ourselves that are sporty, fun loving, creative or even silly.

We nees to discover the lighter side of ourselves

People with religious beliefs also meet together to share thoughts and discussion, worship and praise. This reaffirms their faith. It is very hard to keep up religious belief in isolation.

Think
IT THROUGH

? *If people leave their home community and go to live abroad or in another part of the country, they are often glad to meet with someone from home while they are away. Why do you think this is so?*

Think
IT THROUGH

The development of self-concept and personal relationships

Explaining self-concept

<u>Self-concept</u> describes the image you have of yourself. In other words, it is how you see yourself. You may be content if your ideal image or self-concept is close to your own image of yourself or your own self-concept. Some people have a very realistic concept of who they are and what they are capable of. Most people have an ideal self-concept – someone whom they would like to be or be like. It helps in terms of being content if your ideal self-concept isn't too far from your actual self-concept. It is useful to try to understand something of your own identity or self-concept if you work as a carer because it will affect what you say and do in relation to others.

Influences on self-concept

Our self-concept is formed by how people behave towards us and then our response to them. It is a two-way process. We have an image of who we are, and we choose our friends because they are similar to us and like the things we like. In return, they reinforce aspects of our personality that are like them.

Self-concept is important because it can help you to do well at things or cause you to do badly. How motivated you are will depend on how you see yourself.

THE JARGON DRAGON

self-concept – the way people see and think about themselves

Informal relationships help to maintain balance in our lives

THE
JARGON
DRAGON

socialisation – the process whereby people become members of their society and learn its rules

A good self-concept can give you a sense of confidence, make you happy and help you to enjoy life.

Major influences on our self-concept are our primary carers or parents. They help to form our values, attitudes, patterns of behaviour and roles. They are one of the main agents of **socialisation**.

Explaining socialisation

Socialisation is not socialising – you may do that at discos. Socialisation is a sociological term, which is more significant than just socialising – it affects every individual.

FIND
IT
OUT

Find out what the word 'sociological' means.

Socialisation is the process whereby we become members of our society. We are born with instincts to eat, to rest, etc., but we are taught how to behave, how to dress, how to speak, etc. We absorb our 'cultural patterns', or ways to behave, through our parents, friends, education, media and work.

Socialisation starts when a baby is born and only ends on death. People continue to be socialised by the new situations they meet in their lives.

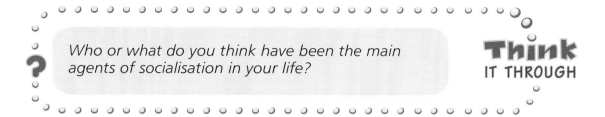

Who or what do you think have been the main agents of socialisation in your life?

Think
IT THROUGH

Roles

We learn our roles through the socialisation process. We absorb by watching, listening and imitating how we should be, what we should say and how we should act. We learn very quickly what is appropriate or right. Each situation has its own <u>norms</u>, or guidelines to behaviour, so that when we first go to school we might rage and kick because we don't want to go. When we reach secondary school we still might not want to go, but we tend not to rage and kick because we know it is a normal thing to do and that it is expected of us.

THE **JARGON DRAGON**

norms – guidelines to behaviour

Think of other norms or guidelines to behaviour associated with:
* *eating out in a restaurant*
* *going to church or a religious meeting*
* *queuing for a bus.*

FIND IT OUT

Particular groups have their own norms as part of their culture. These include the traditions of dress, ceremonies, festivals and norms of table manners and courtesy.

People who are interested in particular types of music may have norms that belong to that group.

Norms and roles may change because of factors in society (for example, the availability of contraception, in the form of the Pill, changed the role of women) and because of influences on health and well-being. Sometimes particular roles are associated with different social class groupings. This isn't very helpful in that it becomes easy to stereotype people because of the social class groupings they may be in.

THE JARGON DRAGON

egocentric – concerned with self, self-centred

Being accepted by the group doesn't necessarily mean that the child is popular

'You can be my friend, you can be in our gang'

Research shows that it is only when children become less egocentric – that is, concerned with self – at the age of about 6, that they develop stronger friendships. Once children are 7 or 8 they are already in roles, which are extremely difficult to break.

At this age it is extremely important for children to be accepted by their friends or 'the group'. Being accepted by the group doesn't necessarily mean that the child is popular. Some children rejected by the group do have friends. Sometimes the child who is popular at playgroup remains popular right through school. Similarly, if a child develops a reputation as a cry baby or a troublemaker, that child may find it hard to shake off that label.

Experiments indicate that children who can pick up other children's emotions or feelings tend to be more popular. Popular children also tend to perceive situations in a more positive light.

Think IT THROUGH

Why do you think positive children and those who can pick up on others' emotions tend to be more popular? **?**

Other common factors found among children who are popular in school include:

- being friendly
- being outgoing
- being the youngest child in a family rather than the oldest
- success in school
- being physically attractive
- often, being tall
- often, being good at a specific task activity, for example sport.

In general terms, girls tend to be more accepting of rejection than boys. Boys who are rejected tend to be aggressive and disruptive, while rejected girls tend to be more anxious and withdrawn.

Self-esteem and self-concept

Many studies show that self-esteem is rooted in family experience. Praise, affection and treating children as responsible all help to boost their self-esteem. High self-esteem tends to be linked with:

- high performance
- good relationships with parents
- greater popularity

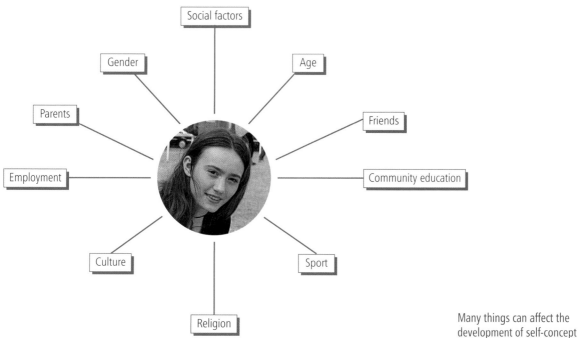

Many things can affect the development of self-concept

- the development of a homing mechanism. This means seeing oneself as responsible for one's own actions and behaviour, rather than being ruled by external forces.

Major life changes and how people deal with them

Everyone has to experience major changes in their life. Change may be painful but it is necessary. If there was no change, everyone would be locked into one stage, would cease thinking, and become bored, full of routine thoughts.

Change is inevitable. Society expects us to change, to take on new, different roles. Even physically, our bodies change in ways over which we have no control.

When we move into a different phase of our lives there may be some awkwardness as we adjust to new roles, new situations and new people. That is why we may feel sad when we leave school even if we are glad to go!

Often the major life events we experience have been anticipated through our socialisation experience. The books we read, the films and TV programmes we watch, the discussions we have all help to prepare us for the next event. So, the first time a girl goes out on a date with a boy there is a sort of script that she can follow – an expected way of behaving.

Times of major change

Starting school
Children preparing for school may be taken on visits, read relevant stories about starting school, walk past the school building and help deliver or pick up older siblings. They will learn to go to the toilet independently and dress on their own. Parents may be around at first. Parents may need to be patient, offering comfort toys and favourite foods, deal with the inevitable tiredness, reducing other changes and preparing suitable clothes, possessions and equipment.

Parents can worry about children not looking after themselves properly

Leaving home

Young people preparing to leave home may take breaks away on their own first. If young people go on to higher or further education there is a natural break, which may reduce the impact of eventually leaving home permanently. In this case, checking out decent accommodation with parents and taking familiar bits and pieces with you may help.

> *What other ideas can you come up with to help you prepare for leaving home?*

Think IT THROUGH

Starting work

People preparing for the world of work may have had some work experience. They may possibly reduce or increase their socialising to give balance or rest, and try to reduce other life changes. They may buy new clothes and make transport arrangements. They will need to acquire knowledge of the job and its tasks, and get to know the supervisor.

Marriage/engagement

Couples who are planning to marry may attend marriage preparation classes or read relevant books. They may take holidays together, spend time listening to each other and spend time with parents, ensuring they have a solid financial and practical base. Research shows that couples who marry with parental approval and have a solid financial basis are less likely to divorce. The following questions may be asked:

- Has each individual been independent for long enough?
- Has each individual reached a satisfactory point in their careers?
- Are they ready to commit themselves solely to each other?
- Is each individual ready to leave their former role of son or daughter to make an emotional bond with their partner?

Parenthood

Couples preparing for parenthood may take parentcraft classes, read relevant books and watch videos. They may discuss the subject with friends. Like most life events all practising has to be done on the job.

Changing jobs

When changing jobs it is often difficult to limit other change factors like moving house and changing children's schools, down to things like changing your car or even learning to drive. Meeting with other people connected with the job and visiting the area may be helpful, if that is possible. Likewise, it is worth finding out as much as possible about the actual tasks of the job, working out social contacts and places to go for leisure to provide some balance in the early pressured stages. Keeping as physically fit and healthy as possible by paying attention to diet, exercise and general lifestyle factors, including drinking and smoking, will also be helpful.

Moving house

If you have an unsettled base for home this may affect your performance at work. If there is pressure both at work and home then your stress ratings soar. Enlist as much help practically as you can and use as many professional sources of help as you can afford, e.g. a full removal service. Make arrangements to see old friends and neighbours. Invite new neighbours round to make contacts.

Moving house can be one of life's most stressful activities

Retirement

People preparing for retirement may take pre-retirement courses, gradually reduce working hours, increase hobbies and possibly find some voluntary work. They need to check their financial security and the manageability of their current accommodation, and hopefully keep in touch with people from work.

Death

The death of a spouse is a very heavy burden to bear. Women tend to outlive men but anyone may find themselves very bewildered when their husband or partner dies. If the couple have followed traditional role patterns where the man has dealt with financial matters and household maintenance, the woman will have to adjust to this. Conversely, some men may find it hard to shop and cook for themselves if their wife dies first.

Changing relationships

Just as we are continually changing, being socialised for new and different situations, so it is inevitable that the relationships we form need to change. Transition times, or times of major change, often test relationships.

Relationships change not only because individuals change and develop, but also because of wider issues – a woman may return to work after a period at home, a man may become unemployed, a daughter or a son may go on to higher education. A family may become richer (maybe even by winning the Lottery!), enabling them to enjoy better transport and holidays, or the reverse may happen and they may become poorer. Both situations may change the relationships within the family.

Family break-up

Tensions exist in families for many reasons. Studies tend to focus on the divorce of parents, but relationships between parent and child or between siblings (brothers and sisters) are very significant and are often linked with parental separation.

However, other factors also play a big part in family break-ups, namely:

- finance
- accommodation
- work
- unemployment.

The possible consequences of family separations are as follows:

- Practically – loss of income, different accommodation requirements, change of job or school, the need to make arrangements for legalities of separation and access necessitating time off work, and reduced energy levels because of the trauma and stress.
- Emotionally – great feelings of loss, sadness, resentment, anger, anxiety, withdrawal, lack of motivation, no drive to make an effort either at school or at work.
- Socially – it may be difficult to see old friends because of their attachments to the 'lost' partner. Former haunts, places of social interest and leisure may become awkward to visit because of associations with the former partner.

For most of his early life Jackson did not see much of his parents and when he did they kept him at a distance. His parents had jobs that took them away from home for long periods. His father was a long-distance lorry driver and his mother was a nurse who worked nights at the local hospital. When his parents were at home they spent most of their time with each other and very little with him. When he was a baby they only had time to put Jackson to bed. He spent much of his life with a number of babysitters and childminders.

Both parents had difficulty showing Jackson affection and he never learned how to give affection or trust to them in return. He never got close to his parents and had difficulty sharing his problems and concerns with them. He felt that he could not trust anyone with any intimate or important experiences.

When Jackson grew up and began to form teenage and adult relationships, he had problems keeping friends or partners. He always wanted a lot of love and affection from them, but because of his difficulty in giving love, the relationships never lasted very long.

Q *What kind of early relationship with his parents would have enabled Jackson to establish more positive personal relationships with people of his own age?*

The more bitter the break-up, the more difficult it is for all concerned to readjust. However, there are many examples of families who have overcome difficulties and have gone on to lead a happy life.

Remarriage

Sometimes remarriage makes new demands on families who have to readjust to step-siblings and step-parents. It may also involve the practical upheaval of new schools and accommodation. Family separations are often particularly painful if they occur while a family member is going through a developmental transition already, such as adolescence.

Reactions to major life events

Experts have suggested that people go through various stages when experiencing traumas, for example, if they are grieving for the death of someone close to them.

The early stages involve denial, shock, numbness and disbelief. There may be questioning: 'Is this really happening to me?'; 'He can't tell me I'm redundant, I've been working here for 25 years'; 'She can't have found someone else – we're married, we've got children.'

Finally, the person begins to reorganise their sense of self and their life in accordance with the new situation and this is very positive.

How people manage change

Despite the possibility of positive outcomes, individuals often resist change, seeming to be naturally suspicious of it. There are a number of social support groups, which may help with change in people's lives.

Family and friends

One of the most important social support groups is the family. It offers support in maintaining the well-being of family members by providing housing and proper diet, teaching standards of hygiene and health care and also caring for those who fall ill.

Recent changes in society have widened the role of the family further. Recent government policy has emphasised a reduced role for the state, with the family taking more responsibility in caring for the needs of its more dependent members. Unemployment, poverty, the increase in one-parent families and the necessity for women to work outside the home have all made it difficult for families to look after their dependent members.

Social support

Research suggests that a lack of social support, such as practical assistance, financial help, information and advice, psychological support, and close social or emotional relationships, can increase vulnerability to illness and disease. In one study, those who were classed as socially isolated were two to three times more likely to die early than those who were part of a supportive social group. Other studies show that disabled people with few social contacts were less likely to improve their mobility than people with high levels of contact with others. The main contribution of social support would seem to be that of a buffer, particularly when people are experiencing adverse life events.

Professional carers and services

The following professionals may be of help to people undergoing life changes.

Counsellors   Counsellors can offer both emotional and psychological support, as well as practical help. For example,

There are many types of formal support available for people with difficulties

bereavement counsellors can help a person to come to terms with the death of a loved one. Financial counsellors can help with money problems.

Doctors – Doctors can help with support and possibly temporary medication to help a person through a psychologically painful period; they can also refer patients to more specialist services if required.

Local Social Services and Education Departments – Local Social Services and Education Departments can also provide practical help and advice in times of stress and change.

Voluntary and faith-based services – Voluntary services provide a valuable service in supporting people through change. Relate (which used to be called Marriage Guidance) provides a counselling service to people experiencing difficulties in their relationships. Cruse is a voluntary organisation, which has been providing services to bereaved people for many years.

Legal and financial advice services, such as Citizens' Advice Bureaux, offer free support and advice.

Local faith-based groups are vital in supporting many people through difficult periods.

Many faith groups are also vital support providers

Sylvia is 80. She married young and lived with her husband until his death at 60, 20 years ago. She now lives alone. She is well educated. Until her retirement at 65, she worked in a bank. For the past 15 years she has worked as a volunteer for a local charity, visiting other older adults who live alone. She has led a very sociable life. She was a keen dancer and is also a very good card player.

Sylvia had three children. One died a few days after she was born. The other two are in Australia.

Sylvia has recently had a hip replacement, which was not a great success. The after-effects of the operation restricted her mobility, and she can no longer sit still for long periods to play cards and she has difficulty dancing. As a result, her social life has been severely restricted.

Sylvia decided some months ago to make an application to enter residential care, as she was feeling lonely. She was also finding it more and more difficult to look after herself after a recent fall. She has lost her self-confidence. The manager of a local residential establishment visited Sylvia to discuss with her the time and date of admission.

continued

case study

Sylvia likes the home. It is democratic. She is able to get up in the morning when it suits her, and she has a choice of meals for lunch and dinner. She likes her room with her personal belongings. She feels safe and secure as she has a key to her room.

Q *Identify the major life changes Sylvia has gone through.*

Describe the help that Sylvia could have received to cope with the major changes in her life.

How did she cope with the transition to residential care?

What would the social and emotional effects of admission to residential care be for Sylvia?

Glossary

Acute disability
A condition that occurs suddenly, which may be severe and may last for a relatively short time. Examples are a broken leg or arm.

Aerobic exercise
Exercise that works the heart, lungs and blood system, such as running, fast swimming and fast cycling.

Anaerobic exercise
Exercise that concentrates on stretching and flexing muscles, such as yoga and general stretch work.

Balanced diet
A diet that provides a person with enough of the various types of nutrient to meet their needs. It does not have excesses (too much) or deficiencies (too little) of anything.

Basic physical needs
Needs humans have that must be met in order for them to stay alive. These include the need for shelter and the needs to satisfy hunger, thirst and sexual desire. They include also the need to maintain temperature, the need for oxygen, sleep and sensory pleasure.

Blood alcohol concentration (BAC)
The amount of alcohol in the body's system, as measured by police when breathalysing drivers suspected of being over the legal limit.

Braille
Words written as a series of raised dots, read by some people with visual impairment.

Care values
The principles, standards or qualities considered worthwhile and desirable by the care profession. It is important that people working in the health and care professions hold these values and apply them in their work. These professionals are described as working from the care value base.

Cervical cancer
Cancer of the cervix.

Chiropodist
A trained professional who looks after people's feet.

Chronic disability
A condition that develops slowly over a long period, or lasts a long time, or a condition that may be incurable, such as chronic arthritis.

Circulatory problems
Failure of the blood to flow properly around the body.

Compulsory referral
The admission to care or hospital of someone against their will. People who are considered a danger to themselves or who are mentally ill may be compulsorily referred to hospital for care.

Conception
The moment when the sperm fertilises the egg.

Congenital disability
A non-hereditary condition, which exists at birth.

Correlation
Describes the relationship between things.

Deficit model
A model that makes a victim out to be deficient in some way and personally responsible for their condition.

Direct discrimination
Treating people less favourably than others because of their gender, race or disability.

Directed thinking
The ability to concentrate on one object or task.

Discrimination
What a person does – how they treat another person or group unfairly, based on their prejudice. (*See* Prejudice.)

Egocentric
Describes a person who is concerned with themselves. A person who is self-centred.

Emotional needs
Need for love, to be wanted, to be respected.

Empowerment
Enabling people to make decisions for themselves.

Emphysema
Disease of the lungs that may be caused by smoking.

Epidemiology
Finding out how many people have an illness or disease.

Extended family
A family that includes grandparents, aunts, uncles and cousins, as well as parents and children.

Gene
Cells containing DNA, which holds the material that determines a person's make-up

Genetic inheritance
Acquisition of certain characterisitics from parents, such as hair or eye colour.

Growth
When discussing human growth and development, this word refers to physical growth.

Health promotion
Advising others about health and well-being. Health promotion materials such as videos and pamphlets may help to get the message across.

Immunisation
See *Vaccination*.

Indirect discrimination
Where conditions are set that exclude certain groups, for example a requirement for all police to wear uniform headgear will exclude a sikh who wears a turban.

Infertility
Inability to conceive and deliver a baby.

Lifestyle factors
Diet, age, exercise and sleep.

Life expectancy
How long a person can be expected to live.

Lung efficiency
How well the lungs work.

Menopause
Stage of life of a woman that involves a series of changes in female hormones. This eventually means the end of the woman's ability to have children.

NHS Direct
A 24-hour telephone or internet health advice service staffed by nurses and trained operators. NHS Direct will give advice and immediate information on what to do and not to do in an emergency – at any time of day or night.

Norms
Guidelines to behaviour.

Nuclear family
A couple and their children living alone as a unit.

Nutritionally deficient
Lacking the correct levels of vitamins and minerals for a healthy body.

Obese
Very overweight, to the extent of risking health.

Personality
Aspects of a person's character that remain relatively permanent.

Personal space
The space that a person needs for themselves, where only those they know well can enter. You shake hands with people you have just met, but you may let others into your personal space and hug them.

Physical needs
Physical needs include food, sleep, warmth, sex and shelter.

Poor personal hygiene
Not washing the hands, body, hair and teeth properly. This causes the spread of more disease than anything else in the care sector.

'Postcode lottery'
Describes a person's chance of getting a health or care service depending upon where they live. If you live in one part of the country you may get an operation more quickly than if you live in another part of the country. When the place where people live determines their access to health services.

Primary Care Team
The first call when a person needs a health or care service. The team includes general practitioners (GPs), nurses, social workers and support workers, such as home carers.

Primary Health Care Trusts
Trusts that plan and deliver local health care services such as general practitioner services, hospitals and community nursing services.

Professional referral
When a person is put in touch with a service by a doctor, social worker, nurse, teacher or when other professionals may assist the person to request care.

Protein
A nutrient found in food. It is used to build and repair cells and tissues.

Psycho-social
Describing problems or issues that affect a person's mental or psychological state, as well as affecting their relationships and social contacts.

Puberty
'Age of adulthood', when physical changes occur to the body because of the increased production of the sex hormones oestrogen in girls and testosterone in boys.

Pulse rate
A measure of the heart rate. The average pulse rate is about 70 beats per minute.

Respiratory
Concerned with breathing.

Risks to health
Anything that might have a negative effect upon a person's health. These things can be physical, social, emotional or intellectual and include poor diet, changing jobs, loss or bereavement or stress.

Roles
Parts (parent, child, mother) learned through the socialisation process. (*See Socialisation*.)

Screening
Describes the system where all persons in an age group are called or recalled for examination at regular intervals, e.g. for cervical cancer.

Sedentary

Literally, sitting around. Used to describes someone who does not do much exercise.

Self-concept
Describes the way we see and think about ourselves. This includes not only our physical appearance, but also the understanding of what kind of a person we are.

Self-esteem
Describes how we value ourselves. Self-esteem is a value judgement we hold about ourselves, which evaluates ourselves in relation to our own and others' expectations.

Self-referral
The term used when people seek help themselves. This may involve support from family members.

Social class
A system for putting people into strata or layers such as working class, middle class or upper class.

Socialisation
The process whereby we become members of society by learning its various ways and rules. Socialisation starts when we are born and only ends when we die.

Statutory service
Service set up by the government under legislation (law). Examples are the NHS and Social Services Departments.

Strategic Health Authorities
New health authorities that replaced the old district health authorities. Strategic Health Authorities have a number of key jobs:

- find out the health needs of the local population
- develop a strategy for meeting those needs
- decide what services are necessary to meet local needs
- allocate resources (money) to Primary Care Trusts
- make sure that Primary Care Trusts work properly.

Vaccination/immunisation
An infection of micro-organisms which stimulate the body's immune system to protect against a particular disease.

Index